332
EME
Bernard King Library
310105
WITHDRAWAL
AF795130

*Palgrave Macmillan Studies in Banking and Financial Institutions*

Series Editor: **Professor Philip Molyneux**

The Palgrave Macmillan Studies in Banking and Financial Institutions are international in orientation and include studies of banking within particular countries or regions, and studies of particular themes such as Corporate Banking, Risk Management, Mergers and Acquisitions, etc. The books' focus is on research and practice, and they include up-to-date and innovative studies on contemporary topics in banking that will have global impact and influence.

*Titles include:*

Steffen E. Andersen
THE EVOLUTION OF NORDIC FINANCE

Vittorio Boscia, Alessandro Carretta and Paola Schwizer
COOPERATIVE BANKING IN EUROPE: CASE STUDIES

Roberto Bottiglia, Elisabetta Gualandri and Gian Nereo Mazzocco (*editors*)
CONSOLIDATION IN THE EUROPEAN FINANCIAL INDUSTRY

Dimitris N. Chorafas
CAPITALISM WITHOUT CAPITAL

Dimitris N. Chorafas
FINANCIAL BOOM AND GLOOM
The Credit and Banking Crisis of 2007–2009 and Beyond

Dimitris N. Chorafas
SOVEREIGN DEBT CRISIS
The New Normal and the Newly Poor

Violaine Cousin
BANKING IN CHINA

Vincenzo D'Apice and Giovanni Ferri
FINANCIAL INSTABILITY
Toolkit for Interpreting Boom and Bust Cycles

Peter Falush and Robert L. Carter OBE
THE BRITISH INSURANCE INDUSTRY SINCE 1900
The Era of Transformation

Franco Fiordelisi
MERGERS AND ACQUISITIONS IN EUROPEAN BANKING

Franco Fiordelisi, Philip Molyneux and Daniele Previati (*editors*)
NEW ISSUES IN FINANCIAL AND CREDIT MARKETS

Franco Fiordelisi, Philip Molyneux and Daniele Previati (*editors*)
NEW ISSUES IN FINANCIAL INSTITUTIONS MANAGEMENT

Kim Hawtrey
AFFORDABLE HOUSING FINANCE

Jill Hendrickson
REGULATION AND INSTABILITY IN U.S. COMMERCIAL BANKING
A History of Crises

Otto Hieronymi (*editor*)
GLOBALIZATION AND THE REFORM OF THE INTERNATIONAL BANKING AND MONETARY SYSTEM

Sven Janssen
BRITISH AND GERMAN BANKING STRATEGIES

Alexandros-Andreas Kyrtsis (*editor*)
FINANCIAL MARKETS AND ORGANIZATIONAL TECHNOLOGIES
System Architectures, Practices and Risks in the Era of Deregulation

Caterina Lucarelli and Gianni Brighetti (*editors*)
RISK TOLERANCE IN FINANCIAL DECISION MAKING

Roman Matousek (*editor*)
MONEY, BANKING AND FINANCIAL MARKETS IN CENTRAL AND EASTERN EUROPE
20 Years of Transition

Imad A. Moosa
THE MYTH OF TOO BIG TO FAIL

Simon Mouatt and Carl Adams (*editors*)
CORPORATE AND SOCIAL TRANSFORMATION OF MONEY AND BANKING
Breaking the Serfdom

Anders Ögren (*editor*)
THE SWEDISH FINANCIAL REVOLUTION

Yasushi Suzuki
JAPAN'S FINANCIAL SLUMP
Collapse of the Monitoring System under Institutional and Transition Failures

Ruth Wandhöfer
EU PAYMENTS INTEGRATION
The Tale of SEPA, PSD and Other Milestones along the Road

**The full list of titles available is on the website:**
**www.palgrave.com/finance/sbfi.asp**

**Palgrave Macmillan Studies in Banking and Financial Institutions**
**Series Standing Order ISBN 978–1–4039–4872–4**

You can receive future titles in this series as they are published by placing a standing order. Please contact your bookseller or, in case of difficulty, write to us at the address below with your name and address, the title of the series and the ISBN quoted above.

Customer Services Department, Macmillan Distribution Ltd, Houndmills, Basingstoke, Hampshire RG21 6XS, England

# Emerging Asia

## Essays on Crises, Capital Flows, FDI and Exchange Rates

Ramkishen S. Rajan
*Professor & Co-director, Center for Emerging Market Policies (CEMP), School of Public Policy, George Mason University, USA and Visiting Senior Fellow, Institute of Southeast Asian Studies (ISEAS), Singapore*

palgrave
macmillan

© Ramkishen S. Rajan 2011
Chapters 2 and 22 © Ramkishen S. Rajan and Rabin Hattari 2011
Chapters 3, 10, 15, 19, 20 and 23 © Ramkishen S. Rajan and Sasidaran Gopalan 2011
Chapter 5 © Ramkishen S. Rajan and Javier H. Beverinotti 2011
Chapter 16 © Ramkishen S. Rajan and M. Shahidul Islam 2011
Chapter 18 © Ramkishen S. Rajan and Venkataramana Yanamandra 2011

All rights reserved. No reproduction, copy or transmission of this publication may be made without written permission.

No portion of this publication may be reproduced, copied or transmitted save with written permission or in accordance with the provisions of the Copyright, Designs and Patents Act 1988, or under the terms of any licence permitting limited copying issued by the Copyright Licensing Agency, Saffron House, 6-10 Kirby Street, London EC1N 8TS.

Any person who does any unauthorized act in relation to this publication may be liable to criminal prosecution and civil claims for damages.

The authors have asserted their rights to be identified as the authors of this work in accordance with the Copyright, Designs and Patents Act 1988.

First published 2011 by
PALGRAVE MACMILLAN

Palgrave Macmillan in the UK is an imprint of Macmillan Publishers Limited, registered in England, company number 785998, of Houndmills, Basingstoke, Hampshire RG21 6XS.

Palgrave Macmillan in the US is a division of St Martin's Press LLC, 175 Fifth Avenue, New York, NY 10010.

Palgrave Macmillan is the global academic imprint of the above companies and has companies and representatives throughout the world.

Palgrave® and Macmillan® are registered trademarks in the United States, the United Kingdom, Europe and other countries.

ISBN: 978–0–230–23845–9 hardback

This book is printed on paper suitable for recycling and made from fully managed and sustained forest sources. Logging, pulping and manufacturing processes are expected to conform to the environmental regulations of the country of origin.

A catalogue record for this book is available from the British Library.

A catalog record for this book is available from the Library of Congress.

10 9 8 7 6 5 4 3 2 1
20 19 18 17 16 15 14 13 12 11

Printed and bound in Great Britain by
CPI Antony Rowe, Chippenham and Eastbourne

*Dedicated to the next generation:*
*Shreyas, Sahana, Eshan and Sarvesh*

# Contents

# Illustrations

## Tables

## Figures

# Preface and Acknowledgements

The world economy has been undergoing massive and rapid changes and upheavals in recent times. Much of the prevailing discussion of the contemporary phenomena impacting the global economy is largely journalist in nature, lacking any solid analysis or debate. Many scientific works are either narrow in their perspective or not easily comprehensible. This book therefore aims to discuss contemporary international economic issues in a straightforward manner that makes it intelligible to students of applied economics, public policy and international affairs, international commerce and so on, in addition to being relevant to policy makers, practitioners and interested observers. The book consists of 25 short essays divided into five parts, dealing with different aspects of international economic policy, with particular – though not exclusive – focus on emerging Asia.

Part I of the book is devoted to *crisis, capital flows and exchange rates in Asia,* with a focus on capital flows into and from emerging Asia since the 1990s (including before and after the Asian and global financial crises of 1997–98 and 2008–09, respectively), the perennial issue of whether the US dollar will maintain its supremacy in global reserves and the choices and impacts of Asian currency regimes in China and the rest of emerging Asia.

Part II deals with *issues relating to exchange rate crises and controls in Asia and other emerging economies.* Special attention is paid to concerns in Asia about exchange rate volatility, the continued interest in some form of restraints on capital flows or taxes on foreign exchange trading, the extent and impact of banking sector internationalisation in Asia, and concerns about sovereign debt defaults, which have come to the fore in the era of the global financial crisis.

Part III deals with *selected issues concerning Asia and the global financial architecture.* It focuses on the impact of the global financial crisis on Asia, analyses issues relating to sequencing of regional cooperation, takes stock of regional monetary and financial cooperation, including the Asian Currency Unit (ACU), and discusses Asia's role in the Group of 20 (G20) meetings.

Part IV draws the reader's attention to *monetary and financial issues in India,* as it is a fast-growing economy that is helping gradually to reshape regional and global architectures. This part explores issues relating to macroeconomic management in the country in the face of sharp capital inflows and outflows, how it has responded to the global financial crisis and the challenges it faces in foreign exchange reserve management. A chapter in this part also explores the importance of remittances to India and its South Asian neighbours.[1]

Part V is devoted to *foreign direct investment (FDI)* – an important and stable source of investment for emerging Asia. It considers the differences between foreign equity portfolios and foreign direct investment flows, issues pertaining to intra-regional FDI flows in Asia, FDI to and from the emerging giant, India, and possible steps to attract FDI in view of the global competition for such flows.

Shorter versions of some chapters in this book have been published as op-eds for India's leading business daily, *The Financial Express*. Dhiraj Nayyar, former senior editor in charge of the opinion pages, persuaded me to write a regular column in the paper, and I would like to acknowledge his support and encouragement. However, almost all the chapters (and op-eds) are based on my more extensive research or policy pieces. I have provided references to these at the beginning of each chapter for the reader who needs or is interested in more detailed information.

This book has benefited considerably from collaborations with my current and former students. Six chapters have been co-authored with Sasidaran Gopalan (Chapters 3, 10, 15, 19, 20 and 23), two with Rabin Hattari (Chapters 2 and 22) and one each with Javier H. Beverinotti (Chapter 5) and Venkataramana Yanamandra (Chapter 18). All four are or have been graduate students at George Mason University. Another chapter (Chapter 16) was co-authored with M. Shahidul Islam. I appreciate their assistance and intellectual inputs, especially those of Sasidaran Gopalan and Venkataramana Yanamandra, who also carefully proof-read the earlier drafts of this book.

I would like to acknowledge the support of my colleagues and the resources provided by my current employers, the School of Public Policy at George Mason University (SPP-GMU) in Virginia, USA, and the Institute of Southeast Asian Studies, Singapore. Lastly, but most importantly, my family members have remained unstinting in their support of my career and have provided me the stability I have needed to remain focused on my writings.

Ramkishen S. Rajan
Virginia, USA, and Singapore

# Part I

# Crisis, Capital Flows and Exchange Rates in Asia

# 1

# Booms and Busts in Private Capital Flows to Emerging Asia since the 1990s[1]

A decade or so after the financial crisis hit Asia in 1997–98, the region once again experienced a severe capital account shock in 2008–09. How different was this boom and bust cycle of international capital flows from the previous one? This chapter examines the balance of payments dynamics in emerging Asia[2] to understand the magnitude and types of private capital flows to and from the region between 1990 and 2008.

The search for higher returns led to a surge in foreign capital inflows into emerging Asia in the first half of the 1990s, averaging about 2.4 percent of the region's gross domestic product (GDP), and peaking at almost 4 percent of GDP by 1996 (Figure 1.1). Structural or trend factors leading to an influx of global capital flows to emerging markets included rapid improvements in telecommunications and information technologies, the proliferation of financial instruments, the institutionalisation of savings and the internationalisation of investment portfolios (mutual and pension funds) in search of opportunities for risk diversification. The attractive growth prospects, along with stable exchange rates, sound domestic macroeconomic policies (actual or perceived) and progressive financial and capital account deregulation in many of the (East) Asian economies were forces pulling capital flows specifically into the region at that time. In terms of the types of capital flow, while foreign direct investment (FDI) grew steadily during the first half of the 1990s, and foreign portfolio flows (bonds and equities) were more volatile, there was a notable jump in the "other" net private capital flows in 1995 and 1996. This component of capital flows includes net short-term lending by foreign commercial banks as well as foreign currency deposits and trade credits.

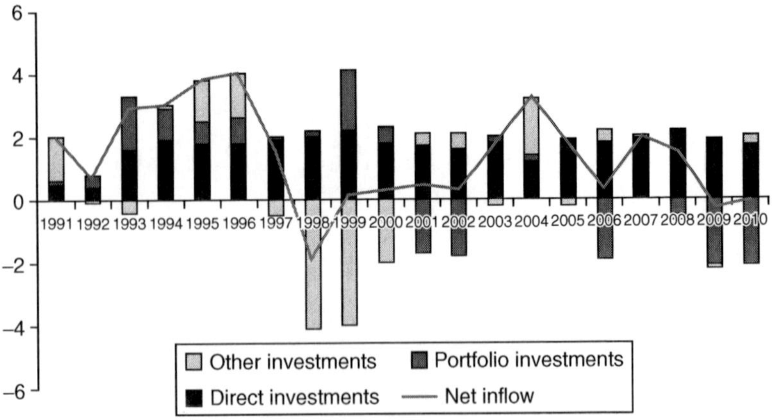


*Figure 1.1* Net private capital flows to emerging Asia, 1991–2010 (percentage of GDP)

*Note*: 2009 and 2010 are projections.

*Source*: IMF (2009). *Regional Economic Outlook – Asia and Pacific Global Crisis: The Asian Context*, IMF: Washington, DC.

The subsequent loss of confidence in these economies resulted in a massive turnaround of private capital flows in 1997, that is the boom was followed by a bust. The data reveal that emerging Asia experienced a sharp reversal in net private capital flows in 1997 and 1998 – net private capital flows dropped by more than half in 1997 (compared to 1996) and then actually turned into outflows in 1998. This reversal was primarily due to the "other" net private capital flows. This component, which peaked at 1.2 percent of GDP in 1996, turned into net outflows by 1998. These reversals in capital flows accelerated thereafter to –4 percent of GDP in both 1998 and 1999 as international banks became unwilling to roll over existing short-term debts to the region. This sudden reversal in bank lending is often presented as strong evidence in support of a bank panic model. However, a less-emphasised feature of this period was the decline in foreign portfolio flows (equities plus bonds) following the initial bank panic, as investors also tried to scale down their exposures in the region. In contrast, FDI flows remained remarkably stable throughout the period under consideration. In fact, FDI inflows experienced a jump in 1998 and 1999, probably driven by a fire-sale of assets in the region as well as greater inflows to China.

Looking at total net private capital flows, the region remained relatively unattractive to foreign capital between 2000 and 2002 for various reasons. In 2000, the reason was primarily sustained outflows in the "other investments" component as the deleveraging process in the region persisted from the previous two years. Despite the fact that these bank outflows finally abated and turned into inflows in 2001 and 2002 – as many regional economies, including South Korea, China and some ASEAN (Association of Southeast Asian Nations) economies successfully issued bonds internationally – overall net private inflows still remained rather modest, largely because of the information technology-induced global downturn of 2001, which led to sharp foreign portfolio capital outflows as well as a slowdown in FDI inflows from their 1998–99 peak.

By 2003, after a prolonged period of restructuring and deleveraging, emerging Asia finally recovered from the Asian crisis of 1997–98. While there was a resurgence in net capital inflows to the region between 2003 and 2005, total net private capital inflows were still well below the average of the pre-crisis period (1990–96). This is true even if one excludes the massive booms in 1995 and 1996, where one might reasonably argue there was somewhat of an artificial surge in "other investments" to Thailand and other economies, driven by the "carry trade" phenomenon (that is, borrow in low interest countries such as Japan and invest in higher yielding assets in Thailand). The primary reason for this difference in the magnitude of total net capital flows in the two periods appears to be the relative slowdown in net foreign portfolio inflows in the post-crisis period compared to the pre-crisis. This is despite the surges in equity inflows to countries such as China and India.

The heightened risk aversion worldwide, especially following the collapse of Lehman Brothers and near collapse of AIG in September 2008, also led to an abrupt about-turn in gross capital outflows from all emerging economies. Looking at net capital flows data (Figure 1.1), while the 1997–98 bust was due largely to the reversal in short-term bank loans, the crisis in 2008–09 was driven somewhat more by sharp reversals in foreign portfolio flows, though inevitably there were also retrenchments by many international banks in response to the financial stresses faced in their headquarters in the United States and Europe.[3]

Overall, Asia has clearly not been buffeted by the global economic slump and dislocations (see Chapter 11). However, Asia (unlike, for instance, Eastern Europe) has done many things right since the 1997–98 crisis: choices that have reduced the extent of structural damage from the global financial crisis (GFC). Asia's relative strength from a macro and financial perspective is apparent from Table 1.1, which is based on six key indicators. The IMF has determined the cut-off values for these indicators (i.e. anything higher is considered problematic) as

*Table 1.1* Macro and financial indicators in selected emerging economies

| | Current account balance[a] (percent of GDP) | External debt refinancing needs in 2009[b] (percent of reserves) | Net external position vis-à-vis BIS reporting banks[c] (percent of GDP) | Average real credit growth over the last five years[d] (percent, y-o-y) | Loan/ deposit[e] (ratio) | Foreign exchange share of total loans (percent of total loans) |
|---|---|---|---|---|---|---|
| **Europe** | | | | | | |
| Bulgaria | **–12.3** | **132** | **–34.9** | **35.9** | **1.3** | **66.9** |
| Croatia | **–6.5** | **136** | **–44.5** | 13.1 | **1.1** | **62** |
| Czech Republic | –2.8 | 89 | **–13.1** | 16 | 0.8 | 13.6 |
| Estonia | **–6.3** | **346** | **–68.8** | 27.3 | **2.1** | **85.3** |
| Hungary | –3.9 | **101** | **–50.2** | 14.3 | **1.4** | **65.7** |
| Kazakhstan | **–6.4** | 82 | –5.1 | **50.1** | **1.7** | 43.6 |
| Latvia | **–6.7** | **331** | **–57.6** | **38.4** | **2.8** | **89.3** |
| Lithuania | –4 | **204** | **–41.5** | **43.2** | **2** | **64** |
| Poland | **–4.9** | **141** | **–15.4** | 14.7 | **1.1** | 32.6 |
| Romania | **–7.5** | **127** | **–32.5** | **47.1** | **1.3** | **55.5** |
| Russia | 0.2 | 34 | 3.1 | **34.5** | **1.3** | 15.3 |
| Serbia | **–12.2** | N.A. | **–12.2** | 26.2 | **1.2** | **68** |
| Turkey | –1.1 | **110** | **–11.9** | 29.8 | 0.7 | 28.9 |
| Ukraine | 0.6 | **117** | **–10.3** | **47.5** | **2** | **59.5** |
| **Asia** | | | | | | |
| China | 10.3 | 14 | 0.7 | 11.3 | 0.8 | N.A. |
| India | –2.5 | 33 | –8.9 | 18.2 | 0.8 | N.A. |
| Indonesia | –0.4 | 73 | –7.5 | 15.1 | 0.8 | 19.8 |
| South Korea | 2.9 | 93 | **–18.9** | 6.3 | **1.2** | 8.5 |
| Malaysia | 12.9 | 23 | –8.3 | 5.2 | 0.9 | N.A. |
| Pakistan | **–5.9** | 28 | 2.4 | 13.5 | 0.7 | N.A. |
| Philippines | 2.3 | 39 | –2.2 | N.A. | N.A. | N.A. |
| Thailand | 0 | 34 | 1.3 | 2.6 | **1** | N.A. |
| Vietnam | **–4.8** | 8 | –7.4 | 26.4 | **1.1** | 21.2 |
| **Latin America** | | | | | | |
| Argentina | 2.3 | 85 | 2.5 | 14.6 | 0.7 | 15.8 |
| Brazil | –1.8 | 40 | –7.1 | 15.9 | 0.8 | N.A. |
| Chile | –4.8 | **119** | –7.2 | 11.6 | **1.4** | N.A. |
| Colombia | –3.9 | 52 | 0.5 | 16 | **2** | 6.3 |
| Mexico | –2.5 | 64 | –2.1 | 11.7 | 0.8 | 11.6 |
| Peru | –3.3 | 27 | –2.2 | 8.2 | 0.9 | **57.5** |
| Venezuela | –0.4 | 59 | 19.7 | **45.8** | 0.8 | < 0.5 |

Continued

*Notes*: Entries in bold in the table point to areas of potential concern. N.A. – Not available.
[a] Projections of the current account balance and GDP for 2009 in dollar terms from the IMF *World Economic Outlook*.
[b] Short-term debt at initial maturity at end-2008 plus amortisations on medium- and long-term debt during 2009, estimated by IMF staff. Care should be taken in interpreting the figures, as circumstances differ between countries. For instance, the figures include obligations resulting from lending by foreign parent banks to domestic subsidiary banks, so the stability of the relationship between parents and subsidiaries needs to be taken into account. In addition, some countries have sovereign wealth funds whose assets may not be included in reserves.
[c] Data on external positions of reporting banks vis-à-vis individual countries and all sectors from the BIS, as of September 2008.
[d] Average growth of credit to the private sector, adjusted for inflation.
[e] Credit to the private sector relative to demand, time, saving and foreign currency deposits.

*Source*: Adapted from International Monetary Fund (IMF) (2009). *Global Financial Stability Report*, IMF: Washington, DC.

follows:[4] "current account balance below –5 percent of GDP; refinancing needs in excess of 100 percent of reserves; net external liabilities to BIS reporting banks above 10 percent of GDP; average real growth of credit to the private sector greater than 30 percent year-on-year; loan-to-deposit ratio exceeding 1; and foreign currency-denominated loans exceeding 50 percent of total loans". While one could argue about the exact cut-off values as well as the indicators used, and could certainly include other indicators – such as those pertaining to reserves adequacy, asset price appreciations (real exchange rates, property prices, etc), household indebtedness, fiscal deficit and measures of liquidity and solvency of the corporate and financial sector – they are nevertheless quite helpful in getting a sense of the potential vulnerability of a country.

As Table 1.1 indicates, with a few exceptions, Asia appears well outside the zone of vulnerability. It is not surprising, therefore, that the GFC has not had as severe an impact on Asia as it has on the other regions. In fact, positive signs – the so-called green shoots – are already emerging, with the thawing of credit markets, declining risk aversion, stabilisation of output and trade, and recovery in international capital flows into the region, especially for countries such as India and South Korea. While the economic recovery in emerging Asia has clearly outpaced the rest of world, the prolonged structural changes and deleveraging that must happen in the United States and Europe are a concern. If emerging Asia is to hope to return to a period of sustained robust growth, it must place greater emphasis on generating domestic and regional demand. This in turn necessitates significant boosts in consumption and investment, which will almost inevitably mean a decline in regional current account surpluses and possibly a recycling of a greater share of external surpluses to the rest of the region. Promising investment opportunities in the region abound, with fast-growing Asian countries, such as India, needing massive infusions of new investments in infrastructure and supporting facilities over the coming years.

# 2

# Asia As a Source of Capital[1]

*(with Rabin Hattari)*

Moving beyond the immediate concerns of the global financial crisis (GFC) of 2008–09, on a more structural basis, there is an interesting fact about capital flows to emerging Asia which is often overlooked but which is of significant relevance to Asia and the global economy. As discussed in Chapter 1, between 2003 and 2006, while net private capital inflows returned to Asia, their levels remained below those of the pre-crisis period (1990–96) average, primarily because of a relative slowdown in the net foreign portfolio inflows in the post-crisis period compared to the pre-crisis. What was the reason for this relatively disappointing performance in net capital flows to emerging Asia as a whole?

To explain this apparent conundrum, one needs to go behind the *net* private capital flows data to consider *gross* private capital inflows and outflows. It is readily apparent from Table 2.1a that across all types of capital, the region received more gross inflows post-crisis compared to the pre-crisis period. Notably, however, the region also experienced much greater gross outflows of all types of capital post-crisis. As is clear from Table 2.1b, these outflows were particularly large in the case of portfolio flows as well as other investments (especially in the form of foreign currency deposits). Clearly some of these outflows might have been recycled intra-regionally, while the rest were invested outside the region. The bulk of the Asian central banks outflows have been channelled into United States (US) government securities – typically US Treasuries (see Chapter 3), since the mid-2000s, many other capital-exporting developing countries consciously began to look for more systematic ways of raising returns on their international reserves on a longer-term basis. More aggressive outward investments by emerging Asian economies in 2006 and 2007 are apparent from the data, especially in the case of portfolio flows.

*Table 2.1a* Gross private capital inflows to emerging Asia and other emerging economies, 1990–2007 (in billions of US dollars)

| | Annual Averages | | | | |
|---|---|---|---|---|---|
| | 1990–97 | 2002–06 | 2005 | 2006 | 2007 |
| **Emerging market economies**[a] | | | | | |
| Total inflows | 210 | 456 | 599 | 824 | 1347 |
| Direct investment | 81 | 220 | 270 | 332 | 400 |
| Portfolio investment | 70 | 94 | 127 | 164 | 432 |
| Equity | 24 | 54 | 71 | 95 | 193 |
| Debt | 47 | 40 | 57 | 69 | 239 |
| Other investment | 60 | 142 | 202 | 328 | 515 |
| Banks | 27 | 67 | 77 | 176 | 231 |
| Other sectors | 33 | 75 | 124 | 152 | 284 |
| Memo: Current account balance | –58 | 252 | 349 | 453 | 507 |
| Change in reserves | –54 | –382 | –470 | –603 | –1040 |
| Official inflows | –20 | –24 | –28 | –45 | ... |
| **Emerging Asia**[b] | | | | | |
| Total inflows | 102 | 221 | 270 | 375 | 681 |
| Direct investment | 46 | 106 | 130 | 145 | 154 |
| Portfolio investment | 20 | 55 | 66 | 90 | 350 |
| Equity | 10 | 38 | 46 | 60 | ... |
| Debt | 11 | 17 | 20 | 30 | ... |
| Other investment | 36 | 61 | 74 | 140 | 177 |
| Banks | 16 | 30 | 21 | 88 | ... |
| Other sectors | 20 | 31 | 53 | 51 | ... |
| Memo: Current account balance | –13 | 170 | 202 | 319 | 445 |
| Change in Reserves[c] | –34 | –247 | –264 | –353 | –641 |
| Official Inflows | 4 | –5 | –5 | –2 | ... |

*Notes*: "Other sectors" comprises non-financial corporations, insurance companies, pension funds, other non-depository financial intermediaries, private non-profit institutions and households.

[a] Comprises the regions below plus Russia, Saudi Arabia and South Africa.

[b] China, India, Indonesia, Malaysia, the Philippines, Singapore, South Korea, and Thailand.

[c] A minus sign indicates an increase.

*Source*: D. Mihaljek (2008). "The Financial Stability Implications of Increased Capital Flows for Emerging Market Economies," Bank for International Settlements, mimeo.

*Table 2.1b* Gross private capital outflows from emerging Asia and other emerging economies, 1990–2007 (billions of US dollars)

| | Annual averages | | | | |
|---|---|---|---|---|---|
| | 1990–97 | 2002–06 | 2005 | 2006 | 2007 |
| **Emerging market economies**[a] | | | | | |
| Total outflows | 76 | 327 | 435 | 681 | 830 |
| Direct investment | 16 | 68 | 71 | 157 | 182 |
| Portfolio investment | 17 | 118 | 159 | 283 | 400 |
| Equity | 8 | 25 | 28 | 48 | 69 |
| Debt | 9 | 93 | 131 | 235 | 331 |
| Other investment | 40 | 143 | 212 | 251 | 248 |
| Banks | 20 | 44 | 73 | 116 | 124 |
| Other sectors | 17 | 99 | 140 | 135 | 124 |
| Memo: official outflows | 0 | –3 | –6 | 2 | ... |
| **Emerging Asia**[b] | | | | | |
| Total outflows | 51 | 139 | 177 | 316 | 502 |
| Direct investment | 10 | 26 | 30 | 54 | 77 |
| Portfolio investment | 9 | 57 | 58 | 166 | 335 |
| Equity | 6 | 15 | 17 | 31 | ... |
| Debt | 3 | 42 | 42 | 135 | ... |
| Other investment | 29 | 58 | 97 | 105 | 90 |
| Banks | 13 | 21 | 44 | 47 | ... |
| Other sectors | 13 | 38 | 53 | 59 | ... |
| Memo: official outflows | 1 | 1 | 0 | 2 | ... |

*Notes*: "Other sectors" comprises non-financial corporations, insurance companies, pension funds, other non-depository financial intermediaries, private non-profit institutions and households.

[a] Comprises the regions below plus Russia, Saudi Arabia and South Africa.

[b] Asia comprises China, India, Indonesia, Malaysia, the Philippines, Singapore, South Korea and Thailand.

*Source*: D. Mihaljek (2008). "The Financial Stability Implications of Increased Capital Flows for Emerging Market Economies". Bank for International Settlements, mimeo.

Despite the relatively lower capital account surpluses in the region as a whole, emerging Asian economies accumulated reserves at record levels, due largely to the persistent current account surpluses accumulated by many of the regional economies (India, South Korea and Vietnam ran up current account deficits). But where were the gross outflows from Asia destined for?

There is no comprehensive data available that can help us to understand where the Asian monies were heading. However, in the specific case of gross foreign asset purchases in the US – presumably a major destination – the Treasury International Capital (TIC) Reporting System data provides a very useful clue about the countries in Asia and elsewhere that were investing in the US, and the types of investments involved. While the country coverage of the TIC data is quite extensive (including 40 countries in the broad Asia-Pacific region), there are some important limitations to the TIC data that need to be borne in mind.

First, like balance of payments data in general, the TIC data is based on the proximate source, not the originating source. This implies that some investments from Asia to the US that are transshipped via non-Asian intermediaries (such as London and offshore financial centres) would not be attributed to Asia. Second, the data does not break down the source of inflows by their status as official (that is, central banks), quasi-official (from sovereign wealth funds (SWFs) or government-linked companies), or private.[2] Third, while data is available on both a monthly and an annual basis, the latter is far more accurate, not only being based on a comprehensive benchmark survey of foreign holdings of US portfolio assets, but more easily compiled on a regional basis, though it is only available with a year's lag on a stock basis. Thus, given its accuracy, we use the annual data.[3] Finally, the TIC data is limited to portfolio transactions, that is, marketable debt (Treasury, corporate and agency bonds) and portfolio equity as well as other short-term derivatives. It excludes bank flows and FDI, though these are not very important net sources of external finance to the US.

What does the data tell us? Figure 2.1 highlights the growth in portfolio capital inflows into the US. While the shares of the various inflows have been fairly stable, the increase in corporate bond and agency bonds in particular – bonds of government sponsored entities (GSEs) like Fannie Mae and Freddie Mac – is noticeable in 2007–08. In general, the US current account has been financed more via foreigners purchasing debt rather than equities. But who is doing the purchasing?

Figure 2.2 shows that Asia's (Japan plus emerging Asia) share of capital flows to the US averaged just over 25 percent between 2002 and 2008.[4] About 40 percent of foreign asset purchases have been due to the developed world (excluding Japan) and the remainder from oil producers and offshore financial centres (OFCs) such as the Cayman Islands. As noted, it is likely that some of Asia's share is understated because of transshipping via non-Asian intermediaries. In terms of investments in US assets, Japan, China and the UK are the largest investors in the US (Table 2.2).

Figure 2.3 emphasises the clear preference that Asia has for US Treasuries and agency bonds. This suggests a degree of risk aversion among Asian

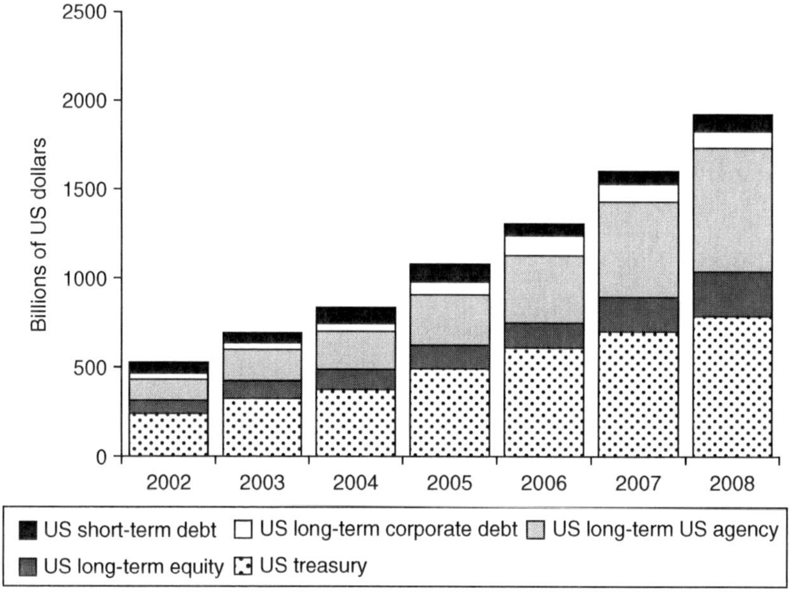


*Figure 2.1* Foreign holdings of US securities by type of securities (billions of US dollars)

*Source*: CEIC Data Ltd, based on data from US Treasury Department's TIC database.

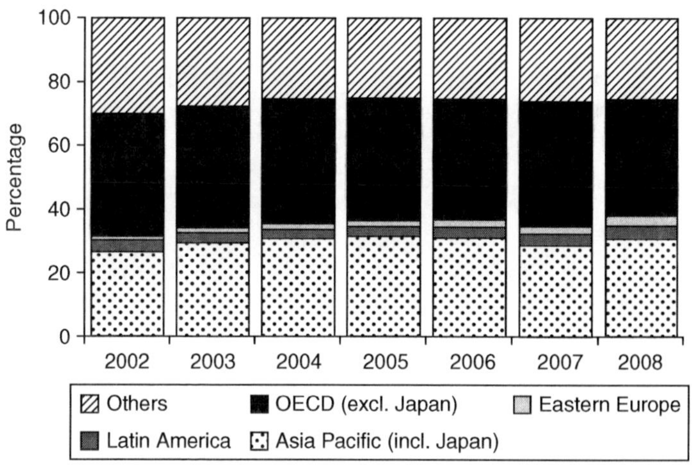


*Figure 2.2* Foreign holdings of US securities: breakdown by region as share of total (percentage)

*Source*: CEIC Data Ltd, based on data from US Treasury Department's TIC database.

*Table 2.2* Top 15 investors in US assets, average 2006–08

| | Shares (average 2006–08) | Rank |
|---|---|---|
| Japan | 12.75 | 1 |
| China | 10.14 | 2 |
| United Kingdom | 8.70 | 3 |
| Cayman Islands | 7.38 | 4 |
| Luxembourg | 6.85 | 5 |
| Canada | 4.66 | 6 |
| Belgium | 4.25 | 7 |
| Ireland | 3.50 | 8 |
| Middle East oil exporters | 3.38 | 9 |
| Netherlands | 3.28 | 10 |
| Switzerland | 3.25 | 11 |
| Germany | 2.60 | 12 |
| Bermuda | 2.35 | 13 |
| *Others* | *2.20* | *14* |
| France | 2.18 | 15 |
| Singapore | 1.79 | 16 |

*Source*: CEIC Data Ltd based on data from US Treasury Department's TIC database.

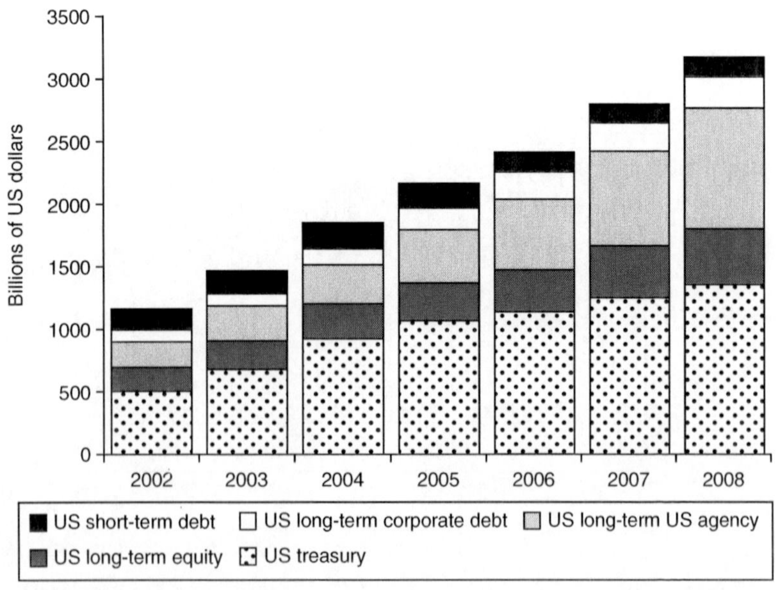


*Figure 2.3* Foreign holdings of US securities by Asia (including Japan) (billions of US dollars)

*Source*: CEIC Data Ltd based on data from US Treasury Department's TIC database.

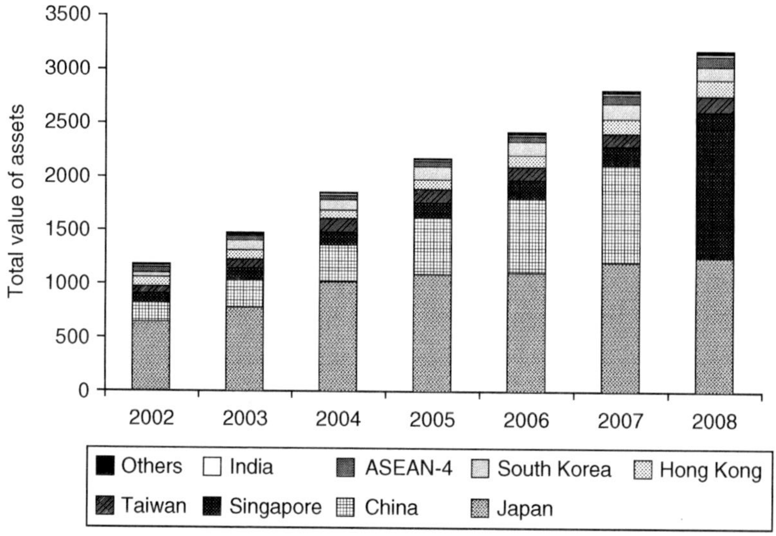


*Figure 2.4* Asian country breakdown of US securities (billions of USD)

*Source*: CEIC Data Ltd, based on data from US Treasury Department's TIC database.

investors and also likely points to the fact that a large source of funds from Asia is central bank reserves, particularly from China and Japan (Figure 2.4). These two Asian giants together constituted 75 percent of inflows to the US during 2006–08, with China's share in particular having risen markedly consistent with the aggressive build-up in foreign exchange reserves. Singapore, Taiwan, Hong Kong, South Korea, ASEAN (excluding Singapore) and India round off the rest of Asian investors.[5]

Figures 2.5 and 2.6 offer some comparison of China's choice of investments in the US vis-à-vis the largest non-Asian holder, the United Kingdom. The contrast is stark. While most of the investments from the UK to the US have been in the form of equities, as noted, the bulk of China's reserves have been in Treasuries and agency bonds.

One will have to wait and see if, and to what extent, sustained concerns about the US economy and US dollar will lead to a more aggressive shift away from US assets from the rest of Asia.[6] Until then, the economic destinies of Asia – China in particular – and the US will remain closely intertwined.

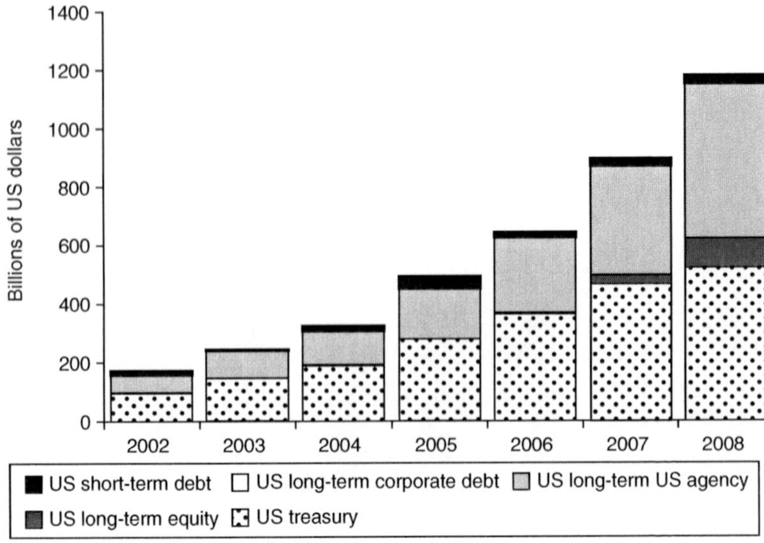


*Figure 2.5* China's holdings of US securities (billions of US dollars)
*Source*: CEIC Data Ltd, based on data from US Treasury Department's TIC database.

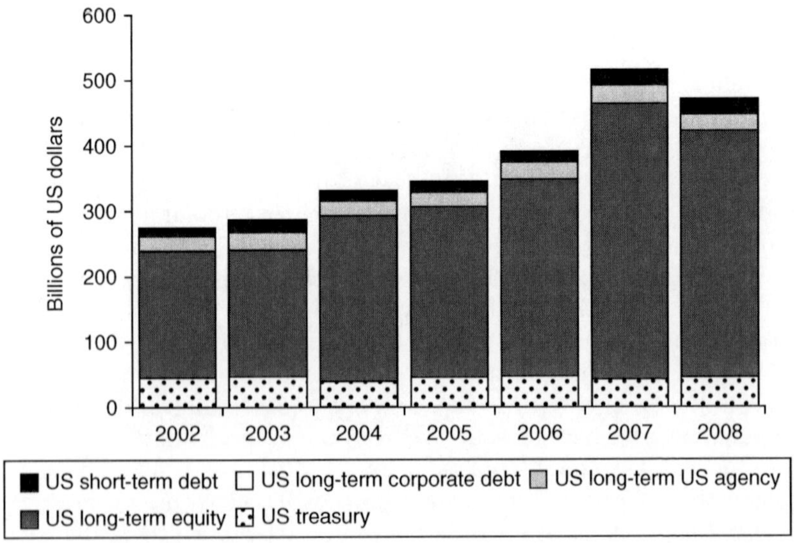


*Figure 2.6* United Kingdom's holdings of US securities (billions of US dollars)
*Source*: CEIC Data Ltd, based on data from US Treasury Department's TIC database.

# 3

# Will the US Dollar Remain the Single Global Currency?

*(with Sasidaran Gopalan)*

Despite the US Dollar (USD) providing the basis for the Bretton Woods system of pegged exchange rates, it has remained the world's reserve currency. However, the supremacy of the USD as an international reserve currency has been questioned and challenged following the global financial crisis of 2008–09, just as it had been on three other notable occasions in the past: during the 1960s when gold reserves were running short, in the 1980s when Japan was a rising star and in the late 1990s when the Euro came into existence. Each time, though, the "USD standard" has proved to be very resilient.

Barring a short period of reluctance on the part of private investors to invest in US paper (especially after the fall of Fannie Mae and Freddie Mac), demand for the USD actually increased sharply once the crisis turned global following the Lehman Brothers bankruptcy, because investors flocked to US Treasury Bills as a measure of "flight to safety".

On a more structural basis, the USD's share of world's reserves peaked at almost 85 percent in the early 1970s. But with the collapse of the Bretton Woods system, the share of USD in global reserves began to decline, reaching a trough of 50 percent in 1990, only to bounce back to about 60 percent during the late 1990s until 2009 (Table 3.1). This time-frame (late 1990s onwards) also roughly coincides with the rapid accumulation of foreign reserves by Asian central banks which chose to maintain a large share of their massive reserves in USD assets. Beyond central banks' reserves, the USD continues to dominate private sector portfolio holdings and is the preferred unit of account for many cross-border transactions in Asia and elsewhere.

*Table 3.1* Share of currencies in allocated official holdings of foreign exchange, 1973–2009 (percentage)

| Currency | 1973* | 1987* | 1995 | 2000 | 2003 | 2006 | 2007 | 2008 | 2009 |
|---|---|---|---|---|---|---|---|---|---|
| US dollar | 84.5 | 66.0 | 59.0 | 71.1 | 66.0 | 65.5 | 64.1 | 64.1 | 62.2 |
| Pound Sterling | 5.9 | 2.2 | 2.1 | 2.8 | 2.8 | 4.4 | 4.7 | 4.0 | 4.3 |
| Deutsche Mark | 6.7 | 13.4 | 15.8 | – | – | – | – | – | – |
| French Franc | 1.2 | 0.8 | 2.36 | – | – | – | – | – | – |
| Japanese Yen | – | 7.0 | 6.8 | 6.1 | 3.9 | 3.1 | 2.9 | 3.1 | 3.0 |
| Euro | – | – | – | 18.3 | 25.2 | 25.1 | 26.3 | 26.4 | 27.3 |

*Notes*: *Data for 1973 and 1987 reproduced from B. Eichengreen (2005), "Sterling's Past, Dollar's Future: Historical Perspectives on Reserve Currency Competition". Working Paper No. 11336, NBER.
*Source*: IMF Currency Composition of Official Foreign Exchange Reserves (COFER) Database www.imf.org/external/np/sta/cofer/eng/index.htm

That said, it is also clear that a serious search for an alternative currency or a set of currencies to replace the USD as the international reserve currency has gathered momentum with the expected slowdown in the US economy over the medium and longer term and the unprecedented build-up of US government debt, financed mainly by foreigners. For instance, after the G20 summit in April 2009, China's central bank Governor Zhou Xiaochuan called for a "super-sovereign reserve currency" based on the Special Drawing Rights (SDR) floated by the IMF. The key rationale for pushing the SDR as an alternative to the USD is apparently to reduce the "exorbitant privilege" possessed by the USD in playing the role of the world's major reserve currency. Enabling the IMF to issue SDRs to quench the thirst of foreign central banks for international reserves would obviously translate into a conscious diversification well away from the USD.

An idea of this kind is, however, nothing new. In fact, it goes back to the era of Keynes in the 1940s, when he proposed the creation of an International Clearing Union that would issue a supranational reserve currency named "Bancor" – a currency based on the value of 30 commodities including gold. Zhou's comments ignited the debate, as did the publication of a United Nations Commission report led by Nobel laureate Joseph Stiglitz, which recommended "a greatly expanded SDR" system similar to the "Bancor" idea proposed by Keynes.[1]

It is useful to note that, at present, SDRs constitute only 4 percent of global reserves, even after efforts by the G20 to expand this pool by pumping in USD 250 billion (it subsequently transferred that allocation to all members, based on their individual quotas in the IMF). Any serious plans to make the SDR the primary reserve asset of the world would require the creation of fresh SDRs of at least USD 3 trillion, in addition to a global central bank authorised to print money. In addition, SDRs can currently be used only in transactions between central banks and the IMF, not in transactions between the government and the private sector. Creating highly liquid markets that would facilitate the transaction of SDR-denominated bonds etc. is not something that could be done overnight.[2]

Apart from the setting up of an SDR-type currency system, quite a few academics and politicians have floated the idea of a few alternative national currencies, such as the Chinese Renminbi (RMB) and the Euro, which could be plausible replacements for the USD in the near future. (The Japanese Yen is no longer considered a serious viable alternative, being essentially relegated to the status of a secondary currency.) While the Euro seemed to be the logical competitor, the severe debt crisis in Europe and subsequent concerns about the viability of the Eurozone have raised several doubts in people's minds about the strength of the Euro as a competitor to the USD.[3]

Given the vulnerability of the Euro, there has been speculation that the only currency that could possibly challenge the USD is the RMB, since China is likely to become the world's largest economy and trader within the next half-century.[4] While this is certainly an interesting point of view, the acute weaknesses of the Chinese financial system and the shallowness of its financial markets, coupled with the non-convertibility of its currency and persistent restraints on the capital account, make the possibility of the RMB becoming a challenger to the USD as the world's reserve currency in the near future extremely remote. Similar concerns rule out other currencies such as the Indian Rupee (INR) for the time being. While India's financial system is considerably stronger than that of China and the country arguably has better respect for property rights, India lags behind China in terms of trade and investment linkages with the rest of the world.

Given the absence of any credible rivals in the near term, it is very likely that America's "exorbitant privilege" of being Asia's and the world's reserve currency will be sustained for some time to come. More realistically, while the USD may remain the dominant reserve currency, its share of global reserves may see a gradual but distinct decline. Over time, though, the world is likely to shift to a multiple reserve-currency system involving the USD, Euro and one or more Asian currencies: RMB,

INR and others like the Japanese Yen, Korean Won or the Singapore Dollar.

This shift is more likely to occur if, first, China, India and other Asian economies continue to grow rapidly vis-à-vis the US: studies have estimated that every 1 percent increase in a country's share of world product in PPP terms is associated with a rise of between 0.9 and 1.3 percentage points in that currency's share of central bank reserves,[5] secondly, if Chinese and other Asian currencies continue to move away from pegging to the USD, and thirdly, if the US fails to regain a degree of fiscal discipline and its economy fails to regain its lustre. As *The Economist* wrote in 2004:

> The dollar has been the leading international currency for as long as most people can remember. But its dominant role can no longer be taken for granted. If America keeps on spending and borrowing at its present pace, the dollar will eventually lose its mighty status in international finance. And that would hurt: the privilege of being able to print the world's reserve currency, a privilege which is now at risk, allows America to borrow cheaply, and thus to spend much more than it earns, on far better terms than are available to others. Imagine you could write checks that were accepted as payment but never cashed. That is what it amounts to. If you had been granted that ability, you might take care to hang on to it. America is taking no such care, and may come to regret it.[6]

If a shift away from the USD does occur, it will likely be a rather gradual process. The military and geopolitical clout of the US (particularly critical in an age of global terrorism) and the deeply entrenched network externalities that are enjoyed by the incumbent will work in tandem to ensure that the USD remains the dominant reserve currency for a long time to come. This point has some empirical validation. A study of the currency composition of global reserves in the 1970s, 1980s and 1990s arrived at the following conclusion:

> We do not detect radical shifts in the currency composition of reserves over time. The choice of reserve asset by developing countries continues to be influenced by a dense web of exchange rate, financial and commercial links with the reserve-currency countries, which itself continues to develop gradually over time. To be sure, there are ongoing changes in these relationships and policies…(b)ut these are evolutionary processes, which again suggests that the currency

> composition of reserves will change gradually, not discontinuously. There are plenty of potential sources of instability affecting exchange rates and the international monetary system. But…instability in the demand for reserves seems unlikely to be one of them.[7]

While the SDR may not rival the USD in near future, efforts should be made to ensure that it plays a more significant role in the international monetary system. One should remember that it was only after the shock of the two World Wars and the resulting devastation of the European economies, as well as the gross mismanagement of the British economy, that the USD was able to assume the role of the world's reserve currency, thus breaking the *de facto* "sterling standard".[8]

# 4
# Exchange Rate Regimes in Asia[1]

It is now common knowledge that rigid pegging of the exchange rate invariably constrains monetary policy independence. Further, both theory and the lessons of experience with pegged exchange rates have shown that such a policy often loses credibility over time and induces booms followed by inevitable busts and crises. The question is: have Asian countries paid any heed to this?

The exchange rate regimes in Asia cover a wide spectrum (Table 4.1). Many smaller Asian economies apparently prefer some form of single-currency pegging. This is particularly true of Hong Kong (whose currency board arrangement is pegged to the USD), Brunei (pegged to the Singapore Dollar), Bhutan and Nepal (pegged to the Indian Rupee) and Myanmar (officially pegged to the SDR, an arrangement complicated by multiple currencies). In contrast, South Korea and the Philippines officially operate flexible exchange rate regimes accompanied by inflation-targeting frameworks. Thailand, too, operates an inflation-targeting arrangement, though it defines itself officially as a managed floater. While Bangladesh, Indonesia and Sri Lanka also claim to operate flexible exchange rates, the IMF characterises them more appropriately as fixed regimes.

A number of other Asian countries have adopted a variety of intermediate regimes (such as currency baskets, crawling bands and adjustable pegs). For instance, according to the Reserve Bank of India (RBI), India "monitors and manages the exchange rate with flexibility without a fixed target or a pre-announced target or a band, coupled with the ability to intervene if and when necessary". Vietnam officially maintains a crawling peg and band around the USD. Singapore officially manages its currency against a basket of currencies, with the trade-weighted exchange rate used as an intermediate target to ensure that the inflation target is attained. China and Malaysia also officially shifted into

*Table 4.1* De facto IMF exchange rate classifications as of April 2008

| Country | As of April 31, 2008 |
|---|---|
| Bangladesh | Other conventional fixed peg arrangement. |
| Bhutan | Other conventional fixed peg arrangement. |
| Brunei Darussalam | Currency board arrangement. |
| Cambodia | Managed floating with no pre-determined path for the exchange rate. |
| China | Crawling peg. |
| Hong Kong | Currency board arrangement. |
| India | Managed floating with no pre-determined path for the exchange rate. |
| Indonesia | Managed floating with no pre-determined path for the exchange rate. |
| Japan | Independently floating. |
| South Korea | Independently floating. |
| Lao PDR | Managed floating with no pre-determined path for the exchange rate. |
| Malaysia | Managed floating with no pre-determined path for the exchange rate. |
| Myanmar | Managed floating with no pre-determined path for the exchange rate. |
| Nepal | Other conventional fixed peg arrangement. |
| Pakistan | Managed floating with no pre-determined path for the exchange rate. |
| Philippines | Independently floating. |
| Singapore | Managed floating with no pre-determined path for the exchange rate. |
| Sri Lanka | Other conventional fixed peg arrangement. |
| Thailand | Managed floating with no pre-determined path for the exchange rate. |
| Vietnam | Other conventional fixed peg arrangement. |

*Source*: IMF data on *Classification of Exchange Rate Arrangements and Monetary Frameworks*, http://imf.org/external/np/mfd/er/2008/eng/0408.htm

currency basket regimes in July 2005. Other Asian economies such as Cambodia, Pakistan and Lao PDR seem to operate rather ad hoc adjustable pegs. Broadly speaking, the IMF categorises these currency regimes as "managed floaters with no pre-determined path for the exchange rate", with China still more of a fixed (but crawling) peg.

Overall, therefore – barring a few exceptions – most developing and emerging Asian exchange rate regimes are, according to the IMF, either completely fixed (both soft and hard) or fairly heavily managed. During the crisis period of 1997–98 and its immediate aftermath, there was a great deal of discussion on the problems associated with a weak currency, that is, a rise in unhedged foreign currency liabilities. This was the reason for the so-called "fear of floating" both in terms of appreciation (competitiveness) and depreciation ("balance sheet effects"). Some corporates and financial institutions in Asia remain vulnerable to their home currency depreciations, but in aggregate, as these economies have moved from running current account deficits to surpluses and stockpiled reserves in US dollars and Euros, they are arguably more concerned about reductions in capital values with a sharp appreciation rather than depreciation of their currencies.[2]

It can be conjectured that exchange rate policy has evolved towards an apparent "fear of floating in reverse" or "fear of appreciation", whereby interventions have been aimed at limiting appreciations rather than depreciations.[3] Empirical results confirm the existence of an asymmetry in central bank foreign exchange intervention responses to currency appreciations versus depreciations in many developing and emerging Asian economies, particularly in the case of nominal effective exchange rates (NEERs).[4] This in turn rationalises the relative exchange rate stability as well as the sustained reserve accumulation in the region.

This is not to suggest that the policy was implemented mechanically at all times. Countries in Asia – most notably India, South Korea and Indonesia – allowed for greater currency flexibility during the 2007–08 periods when there were fears of commodity-induced inflation. Similarly, a number of commentators have expressed concerns that such large-scale intervention runs a serious risk of generating increases in inflation in the intervening countries, and some have even suggested that such reserve accumulation has played a major role in the creation of excessive global liquidity. Key to such issues is the extent to which monetary authorities can successfully sterilise the domestic monetary effects of reserve accumulation.

Many observers have pointed out that the export-oriented nature of the Asian economies – especially those in East Asia – has given rise to a collective action problem (the so-called "prisoner's dilemma") in which the fear of losing competitiveness leads each of them to heavily manage their respective currencies, particularly in view of the limited flexibility of the Chinese currency. Of course, the dynamics of the relationship between China's real exchange rate and the rest of the region is complex. For instance, while it is commonly believed that a real exchange rate appreciation of the Renminbi would benefit some other Asian economies with broadly similar comparative advantage, allowing them to gain global market share (e.g. India, Vietnam), it could also hurt others in the region, as China's imports from the region might decline as production networks between China and Southeast Asia move elsewhere.

In relation to the foregoing, one observer makes the following forceful point:

> Higher tradable goods production in China results in lower traded goods production elsewhere in the developing world – entailing a growth cost for these countries. Of course, some of these costs may have been alleviated by China's rapid growth and the attendant demand for other countries' goods. But China's large current account surpluses suggest that the alleviation is only partial. These emerging market victims of China's exchange rate policy have remained silent because China is simply too big and powerful for them to take on. And this is despite the fact that disaffected constituencies now encompass not just companies but also central bankers, who have found macro-economic management constrained by Renminbi policy. Hence the third consequence. By default, it has fallen to the US to carry the burden of seeking to change Renminbi policy. But it cannot succeed because China will not be seen as giving in to pressure from its only rival for superpower status. Only a wider coalition, comprising all countries affected by China's undervalued exchange rate, stands any chance of impressing upon China the consequences of its policy and reminding it of its international responsibilities as a large, systemically important trader.[5]

As against this, others have argued that China's growth has been beneficial to other low-income countries.[6] Rather than singling out China, another way of thinking about the issue is that regardless of whether China's exports are a substitute for or complement to those of other Asian economies, there appears to be a prisoner's dilemma with regard to exchange rate policies in Asia, which in turn implies that there may be benefits from pursuing a more coordinated approach to monetary and exchange rate policies in the region.[7] Certainly coordination does not imply straight-jacketing all countries in the region in a common exchange rate regime. Rather than adopting a single currency immediately, East Asian economies might consider gradually moving towards pegging to a currency basket,[8] starting with individual currency weights and varying extents of flexibility around the pegs, with a gradual convergence over time (see Chapter 14).

# 5
# East Asia and the Real Exchange Rate[1]

*(with Javier H. Beverinotti)*

Global macroeconomic imbalances are among the key issues facing policymakers, especially in the US and China, the two major affected/contributing parties. While there has been a great deal of discussion on this important issue the literature has, broadly speaking, emphasised three aspects.

First, whether, and to what extent, the Chinese Renminbi is undervalued, using various measures of equilibrium exchange rates. Not surprisingly, there is no firm conclusion here, results hinging heavily on the modelling assumptions.[2]

Second, political economists and policymakers have tended to focus on the actual trade or current account surpluses of China vis-à-vis the US. The argument presented here is that China's central bank has pegged its exchange rate to the US at lower than free market rates (as evidenced by the large-scale reserve accumulation). This "undervalued" currency artificially boosted its export competitiveness while making foreign goods to China relatively more expensive, thus curbing China's imports from the US (Figure 5.1). The policy option in this case is straightforward, viz. China needs to unilaterally revalue the Renminbi as it is "manipulating its currency"; not doing so would invite retaliation from the US government, such as the bill by the House of Representatives passing currency sanctions against China in September 2010.[3]

Third, most macroeconomists – in contrast to the political economists – would argue that focus on *bilateral* imbalances is wrong-headed; instead, the emphasis should be on *aggregate* current account imbalances.[4] The macroeconomists would generally go on to argue that if a country is running a current account deficit as the US has been, all this implies is that the domestic investment rate of the country exceeds its national savings rate (and vice versa for a country, such as China,

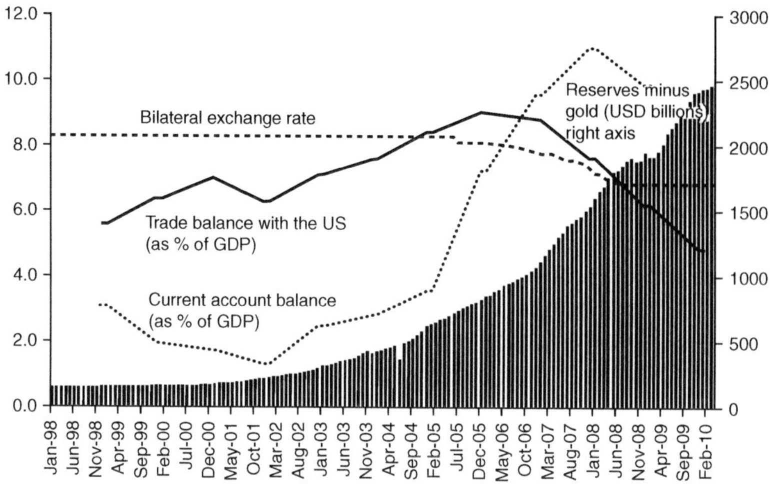


*Figure 5.1* China's reserves, trade balance and bilateral exchange rate, 1998–2010
*Sources*: International Financial Statistics, World Development Indicators and Comtrade.

running a current account surplus). Thus, the appropriate policy focus should be on savings and investment rates in the countries involved. The exchange rate – particularly the bilateral rate – is a highly limited (i.e. ineffective and possibly inappropriate) tool to deal with what is essentially a macroeconomic phenomenon.

So there is a clear disconnect and disagreement between the various groups, causing significant controversy and confusion around the issue. However, what all groups seem to have in common is a general failure to pay sufficient attention to the role of the exchange rate in allocating resources internally between tradables and nontradables, which could have both real and macroeconomic consequences – the so-called "Structuralist approach".

Most economists would argue that the aim should be to keep the real exchange rate at its equilibrium level; exchange rate overvaluation stifles growth and export competitiveness, while undervaluation could lead to inflationary concerns. Thus, one of the goals of many central banks, including the Reserve Bank of India (RBI), has been to ensure a stable real effective exchange rate (in the case of India, proxied as the nominal exchange rate relative to India's trading partners, appropriately adjusted for relative inflation differentials), as any misalignment could create macroeconomic disequilibrium.

However, East Asia's development, unlike that of India, has been rather unorthodox, being centred on suppressing the price of nontradables relative to tradables. This was done through a combination of import tariffs and export subsidies as well as nominal exchange rate undervaluation. This set of policies led to a massive reallocation of resources to the exportables and import-competing tradables sector (mainly in manufacturing), while keeping the domestic consumption of tradables low. This in turn generated significant surpluses of tradable goods, which were exported overseas, especially to the US, thus helping East Asia generate large and sustained current account surpluses (defined as excess of production over consumption of tradables). These current account surpluses in turn were channelled into the US and elsewhere, helping infuse liquidity and keep the costs of credit low, contributing to current account deficits there and thus leading to global imbalances.

The conundrum is why this undervaluation of the relative prices of nontradables persisted: the production of nontradables relative to consumption having been reduced, why was their price not pushed up relative to tradables? This is what most economists would expect to happen, referring to it as the real exchange rate being "mean-reverting". In other words, while policymakers can manipulate the nominal exchange rate, they cannot control real variables.

The conventional wisdom is that the East Asians were able to do this by keeping a lid on the domestic demand for nontradables via financial repression; this kept credit reigned in while maintaining a high degree of fiscal restraint (since government expenditures tend to fall overwhelmingly on nontradables). While this combination of macroeconomic policies was clearly used by China and its East Asian neighbours, given the rapid pace of infrastructural and real estate development and overall credit growth, it would be hard to argue that nontradables demand was as heavily suppressed as some economists suggest. While the nontradable might not have grown as rapidly as the tradable sector, it has, nonetheless, grown quite rapidly. So something is amiss.

Of course, the easy answer is that these countries – China most notably – have an abundance of labour, and this helped keep wage costs and thus the price of nontradables down. This is the "Arthur-Lewis classic dual-sector model" in which wages are set in the rural sector, as the supply of labour is almost perfectly elastic. While this may have been true in the early stages of industrialisation, the data suggests that wages started rising fairly quickly (the "Lewis turning point").[5]

In addition, there is the broader question as to why, in an era of non-commodity based currencies, countries would ever want to bias production towards the tradables sector. The obvious answer here would be that demand for nontradables is limited by the size of the domestic market and is relatively inelastic, while, globally, demand for exportables is fairly elastic. However, the problem with this is that if market forces were allowed to operate on their own, the price of non-tradables would fall relative to tradables, leading to a sectoral resource reallocation without any need for government intervention in the form of currency undervaluation.

Drawing on the older development economics literature, Dani Rodrik has offered a justification for East Asian countries' undervaluation policies.[6] He argues that one must look beyond the static resource reallocation effects and focus on dynamic gains from favouring export-linked manufacturing. These benefits could be in the form of learning-by-doing and demonstration effects that are external to the firm. Thus, markets left to themselves would not produce enough of such goods, and government intervention could jump-start growth via real exchange rate undervaluation to internalise these externalities.

Taking the Rodrik thesis further, focusing production heavily on the tradables sector may also have generated positive productivity spillovers to the nontradables sector, helping to keep its output up and prices down. In other words, the real exchange rate undervaluation may have become permanent without requiring concomitant demand suppression to the degree that most economists might have expected. Of course, stating there may be market distortion is easy; providing specific evidence is much tougher.

But leaving this issue aside, we are left with the question of why should China change its policy stance now if its undervalued real exchange-rate-based development strategy has indeed been so successful. There are a few concerns here.

First, apart from US pressures which may be counter-productive – but understandable as they are effectively "beggar thy neighbour" – the Rodrik scenario is unlikely to continue forever. Indeed, it is generally believed that over time, the productivity of the tradables sector will outpace that of nontradables and wages will have to start rising as the country develops – as has been happening in recent times.[7] This inevitably puts upward pressures on domestic nontradables and thus on the real exchange rate (the "Balassa-Samuelson" effect). In addition, there are the growing opportunity costs of holding low-yielding foreign exchange reserves.

Second, in the absence of rapid growth in the US and Europe, it is unlikely that China will be able to keep exporting its excess production of tradables unless it finds new markets. A better strategy would be to allow for its real exchange rate to appreciate somewhat and shift production and consumption towards nontradables.

So the Chinese undervaluation policy and its hitherto export-led growth paradigm may have reached its limits. Further Renminbi revaluation along with expansion of domestic demand will probably be necessary in future. With regard to the latter, substantial increases in domestic demand in China would require domestic structural reforms, including removing domestic cost distortions and upgrading domestic financial markets and safety nets, as well as reducing the retained earnings of firms.[8] With regard to the former, the announcement by China on June 19, 2010 that it would abandon its currency peg to the dollar and manage the Renminbi more flexibly against a currency basket should be viewed in this context.[9] This said, it is not at all apparent that even if China does revalue the Renminbi significantly over time, the US current account deficit will see any perceptible or significant improvement. In fact, between mid-2005 and mid-2008, the Renminbi rose about 20 percent against the US dollar and about 15 percent in real terms (against a basket of currencies), while China's external imbalances with the US, and in aggregate, rose.[10]

The Japanese experience in the mid-1980s may be relevant here. The Plaza Accord, which led to a sharp revaluation of the Yen, was accompanied by a decline in Japan's bilateral trade surpluses with the US and the rest of the world. However, the overall trade deficit of the US vis-à-vis Asia was largely unaffected, as the US started to run larger trade deficits with other East Asian economies including, and most recently, with China as Japanese manufacturers started to produce final goods from their lower cost neighbours for export.[11] The Plaza Accord emphasises that it is fallacious to assume we live in a two-country world. For the US, what is more relevant is not what China does with the Renminbi. Rather, the US itself must simultaneously take durable steps to raise its own national savings over time, including lowering the unsustainable fiscal deficit.[12] Failure to curb US excesses would merely lead to a transfer of excess tradables from China to a country such as India or Vietnam which would then be re-exported to the US: the global imbalance would probably persist.

# Part II

# Exchange Rate Volatility, Crises and Controls in Emerging Economies

# 6 The Problem with Exchange Rate Volatility[1]

Emerging economies in Asia and elsewhere understand the dangers of maintaining arbitrarily fixed exchange rate regimes. *A priori,* there are a number of reasons that underlie a preference for a greater degree of exchange rate flexibility.

First, the more flexible the exchange rate regime, the keener the incentives for agents to undertake appropriate foreign exchange risk management techniques in response to the higher element of exchange rate risk, while simultaneously reducing the extent of moral hazard which could lead to "excessive" unhedged external borrowing (referred to as a "fixed exchange rate bubble"). The introduction of these transaction costs and exchange rate risks may also help moderate the extent of capital inflows, consequently dampening the intensity of boom and bust cycles (this is essentially a moral hazard argument).

Second, small and open economies are far more susceptible to large external shocks, such as changes in foreign interest rates, terms of trade or regional contagion effects. Received theory tells us that a greater degree of exchange rate flexibility is called for in the presence of real external or domestic shocks. By acting as a safety valve, flexible exchange rate regimes, unlike fixed exchange rate, could provide a less costly adjustment mechanism by which relative prices can be altered in response to such shocks. Fixed exchange rate regimes rely on gradual reductions in relative costs through deflation and productivity increases vis-à-vis trade partners to restore internal balance. This can prove to be prolonged and costly, as was apparent in both Argentina and Hong Kong in the late 1990s.

Third, many Asian economies have diversified trade structures, being dependent on the US, Japan and intra-Asian trade. Thus, in the case of East Asia, institutionalisation of the pre-crisis dollar pegs (via a Currency

Board Arrangement or dollarisation) would not have helped domestic economic performance in 1996–97 (just prior to the crisis) to the extent that the problem was, at least partly, one of loss of competitiveness due to fluctuations in the US dollar and Yen cross-rate.

Fourth, an important argument often put forward in favour of a rigidly pegged regime is that it may operate as a nominal anchor for monetary policy and be a way of introducing some degree of financial discipline domestically and breaking existing inflationary inertia. Studies appear to confirm that hard pegs have consistently had lower inflation than soft pegs or floaters in the 1980s and 1990s.[2] This seems to offer a strong case for more exchange rate fixity (and therefore less flexibility). However, most of these studies do not account for the possibility of endogeneity in the choice of exchange rate regimes. Specifically, we cannot be sure whether a fixed exchange rate actually leads to lower inflation, or whether countries which experience low inflation rates choose to adopt such a regime.

Fifth, pegging the exchange rate also constrains monetary independence. To be sure, it is often noted that some empirical evidence casts doubt on the extent to which floating regimes in emerging economies provide insulation from foreign interest rate shocks. However, a study using *de facto* exchange rates for 100 developing and industrial countries between 1973 and 2000 finds that the interest rates of the countries that operated pegged regimes followed the base country far more closely than non-pegs.[3] A closely related paper finds that small countries with fixed exchange rates are most directly affected by interest rate changes in large countries.[4] All this suggests that the loss of monetary policy autonomy can have significant costs.[5]

Sixth, there is a widespread belief that a pegged regime induces increased policy discipline, as fiscal profligacy will lead to reserve depletion or burgeoning debt and an eventual currency collapse. However, the effects of unsound macro-policies become evident immediately under flexible rates through currency and price-level movements (i.e. the depreciation-inflation spiral). In view of this, one could plausibly argue that flexible rates ought to instil greater fiscal restraint (relative to a fixed regime) as the costs of macroeconomic policy transgressions have to be paid up front. In other words, the key distinction between fixed and floating exchange rates may be the inter-temporal distribution of costs and benefits.

While the virtues of moving towards a more flexible currency regime are many, there remains a discernable reluctance by many countries to adopt such a regime wholesale as has been done by the US, UK, Australia, New Zealand, Canada and the like. Why is this?

Countries with flexible regimes have experienced "excessive" nominal volatility over the last few decades. Given relative price rigidities in the near term, this implies a corresponding fluctuation in the real exchange rate as well. It is admittedly difficult to define what exactly is meant by the term "excessive". However, evidence of excessive exchange rate variability comes in a number of forms. For instance, a number of surveys of foreign exchange market participants clearly indicate that short-term/high-frequency exchange rate movements are caused by "speculative" or "trend-following" elements rather than underlying macroeconomic fundamentals. The problem of destabilising speculation appears to be particularly problematic in developing countries with thin markets (Indonesia's post-crisis experience being a good case in point).

Of course, even if it were accepted that flexible exchange rates often appear to exhibit greater volatility than would be warranted by underlying fundamentals, why might such excessive volatility be of concern? A comprehensive survey of the literature on the impact of exchange rate volatility on trade flows concluded that empirical studies have had "greater success in deriving a statistically significant [negative] relationship between volatility and trade".[6] Beyond trade, there is also some evidence to suggest that exchange rate volatility could have a detrimental impact on foreign direct investment (FDI), comparable to the distortions created by currency misalignments.[7]

Overall, given the heavy reliance of Asia on external trade, FDI and capital flows, the obvious desire by many Asian policymakers to minimise currency volatility (quite apart from leaning against the wind) is understandable even if the theoretical and empirical evidence linking currency volatility, trade, investment and growth is not unambiguous.[8] Among some recent empirical studies on these issues in Asia, one study finds that exchange rate volatility (defined as the coefficient of variation of the monthly nominal exchange rate during the year) decreases the flow of electronic components within East Asia, and goes on to advocate more stable regional currency arrangements to promote East Asian production networks.[9]

While many industrial countries have operated fairly flexible exchange rates quite effectively, they have well-developed and diversified financial systems that are able to minimise real sector disruptions due to transitory exchange rate variations (abstracting from the resource-allocation costs of misalignments noted previously). In contrast, hedging instruments and markets are relatively under-developed in many developing and emerging Asian economies. In a review of the "operational ingredients" of a durable exit to a flexible exchange rate regime, an IMF study has stressed the need to develop a "deep and liquid foreign exchange market".[10] Of course, to some extent there may be a degree of endogeneity, in that these markets may develop faster when there is greater currency flexibility and agents understand the exchange rate risks and corresponding need to buy cover. That said, even if there is an ability to hedge, the transaction costs can be too high to make it an attractive option, especially for small- and medium-sized enterprises (SMEs) over short horizons.

At a broader level, it is always useful to keep in mind that the choice of exchange rate regime cannot be done in isolation. It must be seen as part of a coherent macroeconomic and development strategy. No exchange rate regime will deliver stability if governance is poor, institutions are weak and domestic macroeconomic policy is unsound. Paraphrasing Max Corden, one should not be "too sensational" about the choice of exchange rate regime.[11]

# 7
# Capital Controls: No Longer Unorthodox

Lack of significant reforms of regional and international financial architecture have meant that emerging economies have decided to take things into their own hands. Apart from stockpiling international reserves as a precaution against future capital account reversals and implementing stronger domestic prudential regulations, there has been a resurgence of interest in the issue of capital controls.

In some sense, ever since Malaysia imposed capital controls in September 1998, these policy instruments have never been completely off the radar screen of policymakers in emerging economies. Thailand imposed an implicit tax on short-term capital flows in December 2006 and Brazil experimented with different types of capital account transactions taxes between March 2008 and November 2009 to curb capital inflows and exchange rate appreciations. India and China have continued to maintain selective capital controls and used them as countercyclical tools at times (i.e. they have tightened existing or introduced new controls during booms and loosened controls during downturns).

Most recently, in 2010, South Korea, Indonesia and Taiwan imposed selective but rather tame controls on capital inflows to curb flows of "hot money".[1] Many other countries have also been experimenting with different types of capital and currency controls. For instance, the Bank of Thailand recently imposed a 15 percent withholding tax on returns (capital gains and interest) earned by foreign investors on Thai bonds. The rationale offered for the imposition of controls tends to fall into one of the following inter-related "fear" categories: "fear of appreciation", "fear of 'hot money'", "fear of large inflows", "fear of loss of monetary autonomy", "fear of asset bubbles" or "fear of capital flight".

The Korean case has arguably generated most interest, since it is a member of the OECD and has been one of the most liberal economies since the Asian crisis. On June 13, 2010, South Korea imposed quasi controls by setting limits on currency derivative positions by local banks and foreign branches. This move by the Koreans was also significant because it hosted the G20 Summit in Seoul in November 2010.[2] As part of the so-called "Korea Initiative" for that summit, the Koreans argued for the establishment of a global financial safety net through international cooperation – interpreted by many to mean some kind of international coordination/joint macro prudential actions against "volatile" cross-border capital controls.

Proponents of capital controls have found unlikely support from the IMF. In a Staff Position Note (February 2010), IMF economists came out in favour of capital controls as a legitimate way of managing temporary and large-scale capital flows that might compromise macroeconomic and financial stability.[3] Other institutions, such as the Asian Development Bank (ADB), have also endorsed the new IMF thinking that capital controls can be used as part of an overall counter-cyclical policy toolkit to manage capital flow surges far in excess of an economy's absorptive capacity.[4]

Despite its new-found popularity, however, the literature on capital controls remains less than conclusive. This is not entirely surprising as the term – *capital controls* – is a rather generic one encompassing a variety of barriers. Specifically, capital controls involve constraining one or more elements of the balance of payments capital account. In principle, they can cover foreign direct investment (FDI), foreign portfolio investment (FPI), borrowing and lending by residents and non-residents, transactions making use of deposit accounts and other miscellaneous transactions. Within each of these categories, there is a wide range of possible controls. For example:

a) FDI by either residents abroad or non-residents domestically can be directly restricted, or restrictions can influence the repatriation of profits and initial capital, and the structure of ownership.
b) Restrictions on FDIs can take the form of regulations on the issuance or acquisition of securities by residents overseas or by non-residents domestically. Limitations on the repatriation of dividends and capital gains and transfers of funds between residents and non-residents may also exist, as may "market-oriented" tax measures (such as the well known US real interest equalisation tax).
c) Regulations on external debt transactions largely take the form of ceilings or taxes on external debt accumulation by residents and firms (financial and non-financial institutions). Special exemptions

are often provided in the case of trade-oriented enterprises or on a case-by-case basis, as determined by the regulatory authorities.

d) Restrictions on deposit accounts may be imposed on foreign currency deposits held locally by residents and non-residents, or deposits held in local currency by residents abroad or by non-residents overseas or locally.
e) Other capital controls entail restrictions on real estate, emigration allowances and other forms of capital transfers.

Table 7.1 provides a summary of the types of restraints imposed by developing countries, based on data available in 1994.[5]

There is a large body of literature which examines the arguments for and against capital controls.[6] Rather than rehearse these arguments here, we focus instead on four issues in the context of evaluating restraints on capital movements. Mechanisms for seeking to restrain international capital flows may be applied on a *selective* or *comprehensive* basis; they could be applied to *outflows* or *inflows*; they could be *temporary* or *permanent*; they could be applied *unilaterally* or *universally*; and they could use direct *quantitative* controls designed to frustrate the wishes of market participants or the *price mechanism* via explicit or implicit taxation to influence their choices.

*Selective versus comprehensive:* Curbs on capital movements may be more or less extensive. At one end of the range, there could be virtual inconvertibility on the capital account (that is, comprehensive capital controls). India and China are notable examples in Asia. Nevertheless, it is more typical for a country to impose controls, however selectively, on one or more items within the capital account. Of the 155 countries surveyed, 119 were reported to have imposed some type of (selective) restrictions on certain capital account transactions.[7] Of the 119 countries with some controls, 67 were reported to use comprehensive controls. However, the distinction between selective and comprehensive controls is not precise. For instance, even in the cases of India and China, there is relative freedom for some forms of capital movements (such as FDI). The distinction is therefore one of degree rather than kind. A generally illiberal regime, that is, one with comprehensive controls, typically has a "positive list" of exceptions to the controls. A generally liberal regime, that is, one that imposes controls selectively, is likely to have a "negative list" of items to be controlled.

*Outflows versus inflows:* Restraints on capital outflows are generally advocated for two reasons. First, it is claimed that they slow the speed of capital outflows when a country is faced with the possibility of a

*Table 7.1* Capital controls in developing countries (155 surveyed)

| Category | Number of countries |
|---|---|
| Any form of capital control | 119 |
| Comprehensive controls*: | 67 |
| on outflows | 67 |
| on inflows | 17 |
| FDI | 107 |
| of non-residents | 84 |
| of residents | 35 |
| Profit repatriation and capital liquidation | 34 |
| Taxes on capital transactions | 9 |
| Non-resident-controlled enterprises | 6 |
| FPI | 61 |
| of non-residents | 30 |
| of residents | 33 |
| Security issuance by non-residents | 15 |
| Security issuance abroad by residents | 6 |
| Debt-to-equity conversions | 2 |
| Financial transactions | 78 |
| of non-residents | 41 |
| of residents | 66 |
| Trade-related financial transactions | 7 |
| Deposit requirements for borrowing from abroad by residents | 2 |
| Deposit accounts | 83 |
| of non-residents in foreign exchange | 37 |
| of non-residents in local currency | 52 |
| of residents abroad | 29 |
| of residents in foreign currency with domestic banks | 23 |
| Other capital transfers | 70 |
| Personal capital transfers | 34 |
| Blocked accounts | 24 |
| Real estate transactions | |
| of residents | 23 |
| of non-residents | 30 |

*Note*: * Not explicitly defined in source.
*Source*: P. Quirk, O. Evans, et al. (1995). "Capital Account Convertibility: Review of Experiences and Implications for IMF Policy", *Occasional Paper No.131*, IMF.

sudden and destabilising withdrawal of capital during a time of uncertainty. Second, they are supposed to break the link between domestic and foreign interest rates, because a country cannot maintain a flexible exchange rate regime, monetary policy autonomy and an open capital account all at once (that is, the "impossible trilemma"). Thus, crisis-hit economies could conceivably pursue expansionary monetary and credit policies as a means of growing their way out of debt without having to worry about possible capital flight and the concomitant weakening of the currency. Restraints on inflows serve a preventive function. The aim here is to preclude a surge in capital inflows during boom times, so as to minimise the chances of an abrupt and sharp capital reversal (bust) in the future.

*Temporary versus permanent restraints:* Temporary restraints are seen as a deterrent to excessive outflows or inflows during an "extraordinary" period. Thus, they may be used when a country is faced with the possibility of capital flight, to give policymakers breathing room to make appropriate changes in economic policy. Conversely, they may be imposed when an economy experiences unsustainably large capital inflows, due to excessive confidence in the growth prospects of the economy ("irrational exuberance").

The rationale behind temporary restraints arises from the fear that such capital surges could lead to a loss of competitiveness through a real exchange rate appreciation (sometimes referred to as the "financial Dutch Disease phenomenon") and could create macroeconomic disequilibrium. In addition, the literature on optimal sequencing of economic liberalisation has emphasised the need for reform of the financial sector in conjunction with adequate prudential regulation, to limit the possibility of systemic risks, before attempting to decontrol capital account transactions. Under these conditions, temporary controls may allow reforms to be phased.

Permanent controls are seen as necessary even during "normal" times. The rationale here is that even if all the microeconomic distortions are eliminated and macroeconomic policies are generally sound, there may nonetheless be certain inherent market failures that cause sub-optimal decisions to be made in a decentralised and free market economy. If such market failures occur in a *laissez faire* economy, they may provide a rationale for capital restraints on a permanent basis rather than on an event-specific or transitory basis.

*Direct/administrative versus market/price-based restraints:* Restraints could either directly control market movements, or they could be a market-based mechanism which alters the structure of price incentives that face market participants, thereby inducing them to modify their behaviour. There are well known problems relating to the potential for rent-seeking activities (bribery, corruption and so forth) generated by controls, not to mention the high enforcement costs, the inevitable creation of a black market and the general porousness of quantitative restrictions, particularly in the medium and longer terms. These drawbacks of controls, on the one hand, and their potential for generating tariff revenues, on the other, have generally led economists to prefer cost-based levies over quantitative restrictions.

The limited available empirical literature to date suggests that capital controls tend to be more effective in moderating capital inflow surges than capital outflows, and even in the former, seem more useful in lengthening the maturity of capital inflows (thus presumably reducing the chance of booms and busts) rather than in reducing the actual volume of flows. Any dampening effects on the volume of inflows would be transitory at best, as people find ways to circumvent the controls. The empirical evidence for the effects of capital controls on currency swings is unclear and suggests they depend on the type of controls and manner in which they are introduced.

Much of the empirical research on capital controls thus far has been based on the Chilean and Colombian experiences, both of which imposed unremunerated reserve requirements (URRs) to manage capital inflow surges and price booms. If imposed appropriately (unlike the Thai debacle of November and December 2006), URRs seem to have been fairly effective counter-cyclical and prudential tools and have generated much interest with one caveat – a negative unintended consequence – that they may have disproportionately raised the cost of credit to small-and-medium-sized enterprises (SMEs).[8]

What is new about the recent controls imposed in many emerging markets is that they are mostly (but not always) on inflows, they are selective and targeted rather than broad, and are often deployed on a temporary rather than a permanent basis as part of an overall package to deal with stability. In addition, policymakers are particularly sensitive to investor sentiments and therefore take pains to calm markets by emphasising the limited scope of, and the rationale for, the controls. While the acceptance of "market-friendly" capital controls is fast becoming the new norm, it would certainly be desirable for the G20 to develop a code of good practice for the use of such controls.

# 8

# Reconsidering the Tobin Tax

Political leaders in emerging economies who have been concerned about the volatility of capital flows have intermittently suggested a global tax on international foreign exchange (forex) activities. Such a tax was originally proposed by James Tobin in the 1970s. This "Tobin tax" is essentially a permanent, uniform, ad-valorem transactions tax on international forex flows. The burden of a Tobin tax is claimed to be inversely proportional to the length of the transaction, i.e. the shorter the holding period, the heavier the burden of tax. For instance, a Tobin tax of 0.25 percent implies that a twice daily round-trip carries an annualised rate of 365 percent; while in contrast, a round-trip made twice a year carries a rate of 1 percent. Accordingly, and considering that 80 percent of forex turnover involves round-trips of a week or less, it has been argued that the Tobin tax ought to help reduce exchange rate volatility and consequently curtail the intensity of "boom-bust" cycles caused by international capital flows.

Unlike quantitative restrictions on currency flows or price and administrative capital restraints, the Tobin tax cannot be applied unilaterally, as this will merely lead to a migration of forex transactions to untaxed countries (i.e. avoidance via migration). As long as the Tobin tax is levied on the trading site rather than the booking or settlement site, the high fixed costs involved in developing the human and physical infrastructure ought to act as a disincentive against migration. The top two financial centres (the UK and US) accounted for half of global forex turnover in 2007, while the top ten accounted for over 75 percent.[1] Of course, this could lead to a steady erosion of effectiveness over time insofar as new trading sites ("tax havens") gradually develop and strengthen. (While punitive taxes exist on world stock markets without apparent problems, the only way individual countries can unilaterally impose taxes on international financial transactions is if they simultaneously impose quantitative prohibitions, as in the case of Brazil's exit tax on capital flows, for instance.)

If the Tobin tax is limited to spot transactions (as originally suggested by James Tobin in 1976), this will lead to a tax-saving reallocation of financial transactions from traditional spot transactions to derivative instruments. As such, in order to prevent tax avoidance via "asset substitution" or "changed product mix" it should be applied on all derivative products such as forwards, futures, options and swaps. There is a broad consensus that the tax must be levied at a rate designed to minimise the incentive to undertake synthetic transactions in order to evade the tax (i.e. geographical or asset substitution) or to alter the forex market structure from a decentralised, dealer-driven market to one that is centralised and customer-driven. Suggestions of the "most appropriate" rate of taxation have generally ranged between 0.1 and 0.25 percent.

Proponents of a Tobin tax have often suggested that it may have a useful role to play in reducing foreign currency outflows. In contrast, opponents of the tax correctly emphasise that, with sizeable prospective devaluations, a marginal tax on currency transactions will be completely ineffective. What matters is the expected returns from speculation relative to the costs (inclusive of the tax). In circumstances where expectations of currency devaluation increase, the tax will become progressively less effective. Indeed, it will be in the midst of a currency crisis, when its stabilising properties are most required, that a currency tax will be least effective because of the large anticipated gains from speculation. As the late MIT economist, Rudiger Dornbusch, pointed out in 1998, "[a]nyone who contemplates 30 percent depreciation will happily pay 0.1 percent Tobin tax".[2] The comparison of expected exchange rate change and the size of a currency tax is an important issue that has largely been ignored by the Tobin tax literature. Taking this conclusion a step further, a Tobin tax, or any form of restraints on currency and capital flows imposed in the midst of a crisis, could lead to a self-validating panic and crisis. Consequently such measures are best introduced during a period of relative calm.

The foregoing, along with formal research on the Tobin tax, suggests that an international currency tax ought to be designed as a *crisis prevention* instrument rather than one for *crisis management*. In other words, a Tobin tax ought to be applied counter-cyclically, i.e. stiffened during a boom and loosened during a bust. Admittedly, this policy recommendation is at odds with Tobin (and Keynes before him) and others who recommend the raising of tax rates during a crisis. Nonetheless, it is consistent with other empirical studies on financial restraints in general, which indicate that they are more effective at preventing "excessive" capital inflows than at stemming capital flight. The fact that a Tobin tax is relatively ineffective during a crisis period implies that a tax levied at a "moderate rate" will not be able to defend a regime that is inherently unsustainable. In other words, the discipline of the market will remain in operation despite the levy; it does not advance policy failures.

Sceptics may suggest that such a tax would still be ineffective as a preventive measure, arguing that the elasticity of foreign currency flows is low. Parallels could be drawn with the Chilean experience of management of its interest-free deposit requirement (see Chapter 7), which seems to indicate that the restraints have not significantly affected the aggregate level of capital inflows and therefore the extent of real exchange rate appreciation (Table 8.1 compares the main characteristics of the oft-mentioned Chilean-type reserve requirements with the Tobin tax). Two points should be noted in this regard. First, insofar as the Chilean case of unilateral capital controls is applicable to a multilateral tax of foreign currency flows, studies suggest that the controls do appear to have been effective in altering the composition of capital flows. Specifically, they appear to have extended the *duration* or maturity structure of overall capital inflows (having served their purposes, the Chilean deposit requirements have come down to zero). Second, even if a properly designed Tobin tax is unsuccessful in this regard, it must be because international capital flows are relatively inelastic with respect to such taxes. The low elasticity that limits the effectiveness of the tax in reducing capital volatility increases its capacity to raise much-needed revenues. In other words, if the international finance case for a Tobin tax proves ineffectual, this could paradoxically enhance the public finance case for the tax.

While the quantity of revenues that can be expected to be raised from a Tobin tax is open to debate, what is certainly true is that such a tax may be expected to raise a lot of money. While leakages via evasion and avoidance are real concerns (as they are with any tax), the problem can, as noted, be reduced significantly if the tax rate is low and participation is broadly multilateral. Beyond this, just as there appears to be international political will to stop money laundering, there ought to be a similar will to plug leakages that might arise from attempts to avoid or evade the Tobin tax. The issue of tax avoidance or evasion via tax havens is not unique to the Tobin tax. For instance, the Financial Stability Board has identified unregulated and offshore centres as a

*Table 8.1* Summary comparison between the Chilean deposit requirements and the Tobin tax

| | **Chilean deposit requirements** | **Tobin tax** |
|---|---|---|
| **Motive** | Prevent over-indebtedness | Reduce forex volatility (and raise revenues) |
| **Tax applied to** | Capital inflows | All forex transactions |
| **Paid immediately by** | Foreign investors | All traders (mainly interbank trade) |
| **Paid immediately to** | Central bank (foreign currency earnings) | Global tax authority |
| **Relationship of tax amount to interest rate** | Rises with foreign interest rate | Invariant to interest rate |
| **Relationship to maturity** | Fixed amount (falling with maturity in percent per year) when maturity is less than one year | Fixed amount in percentage terms, falls continuously with maturity (if applied counter cyclically) |
| **Where imposed?** | Single country (faced with inflows) | Must be worldwide or major financial centres |
| **Probable level of tax rate** | Low-to-moderate | Low |

*Source*: J. Frankel. (1996). "How Well do Markets Work: Might a Tobin Tax Help?", in M. ul Haq, I. Kaul and I. Grunberg (eds.), *The Tobin Tax: Coping with Financial Viability*, New York: Oxford University Press.

source of international financial instability. Thus, to reiterate, if the elasticity turns out to be relatively low, the tax may not be an effective financial safeguard, but it could generate a relatively large amount of revenue that may then be used for development purposes, i.e. a financial bonanza. The "sin tax" analogy is also useful in understanding the need for currency taxation to be virtually global. For instance, the significant revenue losses on beer and spirits as a number of Britons made their purchases in France to avoid the excise duties levied in their home country led to the British government setting a cap on the excise duty on these products. Similarly, Canada's attempts at a steep tax hike on cigarettes to discourage smoking had to be revoked in 1994 because of their *de facto* ineffectiveness due to smuggling from the US.

Estimating the revenue from currency taxation is a complicated methodological exercise, since much depends on the rate and coverage of the tax, the level of transaction costs, the elasticity of capital movements with respect to the effective increase in transaction costs associated with the tax, as well as the extent to which it is avoided or evaded. Table 8.2 summarises the estimates from various studies. Given these studies, it may not be unreasonable to assume that a transactions tax of 0.25 percent will generate annual revenues of about USD 150 billion. These are certainly conservative estimates, particularly as the computations are based on 1995 forex figures of USD 1.2 trillion as opposed to the 1998 figure of USD 1.5 trillion. While there is clearly plenty of room to debate the numbers and assumptions used, as the numbers in Table 8.2 reveal, revenue from an international currency transaction tax would be large relative to other resource flows.

Revenue from a currency tax could help deal with a foreign aid "crisis" and assist in halting, if not reversing, the persistent downward trend in aid flows. Moreover, with growing evidence that foreign aid *is* effective when combined with good domestic economic policies (i.e. aid does work in the right circumstances), the global political environment may become less hostile to using global taxation as a way of bringing about global income redistribution aimed at poverty reduction. To use the revenue from a currency transaction tax to augment multilateral aid flows would, in these circumstances, have the appeal of assisting countries that are largely by-passed by private international capital markets. Thus, a policy directed towards offsetting the inefficiencies of markets could also be used to mitigate inequity, i.e. a global tax for global purposes. It is not surprising, therefore, that the proposal for such a global

*Table 8.2* How much revenue can the Tobin tax generate?

| **Study** | **Tax rate assumed (percent)** | **Annual tax revenue derived (USD billion)** |
|---|---|---|
| Felix and Sau (1996)[a] | 0.25 | 290 |
| Felix and Sau (1996)[a] | 0.10 | 140–180 |
| D'Orville and Najman (1995)[b] | 0.25 | 140 |
| Frankel (1996)[c] | 0.10 | 170 |

*Notes*: [a] D. Felix. and R. Sau (1996). "On the Revenue Potential and Phasing In of the Tobin Tax", in M. ul Haq, I. Kaul and I. Grunberg (eds.), *The Tobin Tax: Coping with Financial Volatility*, New York: Oxford University Press. [b] H. D'Orville, H. and D. Najman (1995). *Towards a New Multilateralism: Funding Global Priorities*, New York: United Nations. [c] J. Frankel (1996). "How Well do Markets Work: Might a Tobin Tax Help?", in M. ul Haq, I. Kaul and I. Grunberg (eds.), *The Tobin Tax: Coping with Financial Volatility*, New York: Oxford University Press.

*Source*: Compiled by author.

tax continues to be hotly debated and is suggested from time to time by policymakers as a means of taming global capital markets.[3] However, it should be kept in mind that the aim of such a global tax ought *not* to be to roll back the process of economic globalisation, but instead to ensure that its adverse consequences are minimised.

# 9
# Sovereign Debt Defaults: Concerns and Lessons

Just when financial markets appeared to have turned the corner and concerns had shifted to whether "irrational exuberance" had returned and markets had become too "frothy", the world was blind-sided by yet another crisis. This time it was the November 25, 2010 announcement by the Dubai government that one of the city's largest and most important state-owned conglomerates, Dubai World, was requesting suspension on some of its debt repayments as it restructured its finances and operations, particularly those related to its property development subsidiary, Nakheel.

The problems of extremely high leverage and moribund property markets in Dubai were fairly well known. Like other highly-leveraged economies such as Hungary, Iceland, Ireland and Latvia, Dubai was first affected by the global financial turmoil in late 2008 when its corporates found it next to impossible to refinance some of their huge pending projects within Dubai and asset purchases globally. However, after the bailout by the Abu Dhabi government (through the federal central bank) to the tune of USD 10 billion in February 2009, and a further infusion of USD 5 billion by two Abu Dhabi banks just days before the debt standstill announcement, there was a general belief that the problems – while deep – were largely contained and would be managed within the United Arab Emirates (UAE), and that the other Emirates would not allow a major insolvency in or of any member of the Federation for reputational, if no other, concerns.

Immediately after the debt standstill announcement, there were worries that this crisis could derail the recovery in global markets, at least in other emerging economies and among Asian and European banks, which were more exposed than their American counterparts (the exact degree of exposure remains unclear, however). The corporate default spreads on sovereign debts in some indebted countries did indeed rise, and global financial markets did fall initially. However, the risk seems to have been largely contained, and the Dubai crisis was more of a hiccup in the financial markets; fears generally eased about the direct fallout from this debt delay. Once again, this is not altogether surprising. Many other emerging economy crises – Mexico in 1994–95, Thailand in 1997–98, Brazil and Ecuador in 1999 or Argentina in 2001 – were predominantly regional in nature. Only the Russian crisis in 1998 threatened to turn global, and that was largely because of the extent of leverage of the US hedge fund Long-Term Capital Management (LTCM).

The quasi-sovereign nature of the Dubai debt crisis and the complicated relationship between Dubai, Abu Dhabi and the other states in the Emirates made the crisis rather unusual. Unlike other emerging market crises, there was limited impact on the UAE's US dollar peg, given the large reserve holdings of the Emirates Federation as a whole. This was a double-edged sword for Dubai, though. On the one hand, Dubai did not have to fear the impact of currency devaluations on the domestic currency values of its liabilities. These so-called balance sheet effects have, in the past, had severe negative impacts on many other emerging economies: many of their banks and corporates went bankrupt due to currency mismatches (assets and revenues in domestic currencies and liabilities in foreign currencies). On the other hand, Dubai was not able to depend on the exchange rate adjustment as a means of cushioning itself from the negative shock over time (via stimulating exports and loosening of domestic monetary policy).

In this regard, the Hong Kong experience of 1998 is relevant. When the New Taiwan Dollar and the Singapore dollar both depreciated in 1998, Hong Kong's US dollar peg was faced with a major speculative attack. The commitment of the city to its currency board arrangement implied that it had lost price competitiveness vis-à-vis many of its export competitors, that is, its real exchange rate was overvalued and needed to be adjusted. Given the currency peg, most of the adjustment of the real exchange rate had to take place via prolonged domestic price deflation – Hong Kong faced a very painful period of asset price deflation, declining wages and unemployment over the next half decade.

However, the big difference between Hong Kong and Dubai is that the former was a net creditor whose corporates were leveraged to only a limited extent. Dubai, in sharp contrast, was a net debtor and had to worry about how it could reschedule its burgeoning external debts. The international financial system had not developed a good mechanism for international debt restructuring and bail-outs/bail-ins when it came to bond financing. The fact that some of Nakheel's financing was via Islamic bonds further complicates matters, as the jurisprudence on these instruments is hazy. In the absence of established codes of conduct or formal frameworks for bond workouts, the approach to crisis resolution internationally has been rather ad hoc, muddled and informal. Despite this, international debt rescheduling/restructuring is not without precedent, and was, in fact, carried out reasonably smoothly in Argentina in 2001, Ecuador in 1999–2000,[1] Pakistan in 1999,[2] Ukraine in 2000,[3] Uruguay in 2003[4] and elsewhere. Dubai itself eventually managed to get almost unanimous support from its creditors for the restructuring of its nearly USD 25 billion external debts.[5]

While Dubai World temporarily staved off outright default in late 2009 thanks to a bailout from its larger Emirates partner, Abu Dhabi, the episode highlighted growing concerns about fiscal and financial profligacy in other countries. While many potentially vulnerable emerging/developing economies from Hungary, Latvia and Romania in Central and Eastern Europe to Pakistan and Sri Lanka in South Asia were already under IMF programs, markets focused squarely on smaller developed economies in Western Europe. The four Club-Med states of most concern were termed the "PIGS" – Portugal, Ireland, Greece and Spain (some have suggested the term PIIGS, the additional "I" being Italy). All these economies have been running profligate fiscal policies that have been made worse by the global financial crisis (both because of explicit Keynesian stimulus efforts and also because of a cyclical downturn in tax revenues) (Table 9.1).

Of greatest concern has been Greece, which has historically maintained a less-than-stellar fiscal house (with a budget deficit of almost 13 percent of GDP) and there were growing possibilities that the Greek government would default on its bonds held by financial institutions in the EU and elsewhere. Consequently, sovereign risk premia and Credit Default Swaps or CDS (the cost of buying insurance against the country defaulting) spiked after the Dubai concerns. The markets were initially relieved after the Dubai-Abu Dhabi deal, there being a general expectation that Greece and others would also be bailed out in some manner by their partners in the EU. However, the initial mixed signals emanating from EU leaders and the inability/unwillingness of Greece (and Portugal) to adopt aggressive measures to restore fiscal discipline by slashing expenditures and broadening the tax base led to simmering concerns, which started boiling over once again in early February 2010.[6]

As these concerns about Greece and Portugal started to spread elsewhere, with even corporate bond spreads in the US rising and funds

*Table 9.1* Government debt and external debt of PIIGS, end 2009

| Country | General government gross debt (GGGD) *(percentage of GDP)* | General government balance *(percentage of GDP)* | Gross external debt position *(percentage of GDP)* | Net external debt position (–for net credit) *(percentage of GDP)* | General government net external debt *(percentage of GGGD)* |
|---|---|---|---|---|---|
| Portugal | 77.2 | –9.3 | 232.7 | 88.6 | 74.9 |
| Ireland | 64.5 | –11.7 | 979.4 | 75.1 | 70.6 |
| Greece | 113.4 | –12.7 | 168.2 | 82.5 | 78.9 |
| Spain | 55.2 | –11.4 | 168.1 | 80.6 | 47.3 |
| Italy | 115.1 | –5.3 | 117.5 | 37.3 | 42.9 |
| Memo: Germany | 72.5 | –3.2 | 148.2 | –21.7 | 48.5 |

*Source*: R. Cabral (2010). "The PIGS' External Debt Problem", Vox-EU, May 8.

swiftly fleeing from risky assets into gold and US dollars. The rapidly worsening situation and its growing drag on the rest of the region forced the hand of EU leaders, who reached a USD 145 billion deal on bailing out Greece along with the IMF, which required sharp fiscal adjustments by the country. Valid concerns remain about the possible negative effects of bail-outs in the EU on moral hazard and regional cohesion.

While there are a number of outstanding concerns, what the Western European crisis suggests is that, as economies and capital markets become more globalised, countries looking to form monetary unions cannot afford to ignore the fiscal side – a single currency union is probably incompatible with fiscal fragmentation over time, something that the EU has hitherto tried to maintain. From the perspective of individual well-run countries, though, this fiscal harmonisation will further tie their hands, making them less able to deal with country-specific shocks and making the costs of membership in the Eurozone prohibitively high, while at the other end, those with weaker policies and rising unemployment may be tempted to use competitive devaluations by leaving the union.

This makes an obvious but important point for regions such as Asia, which have often discussed the possibility of an EU-type union. An economic union is as strong as its weakest member and, while the initial belief was that membership of the EU would lead to a convergence (i.e. an upgrading) of macroeconomic policies and standards to those of Germany, the reality in some cases has been quite different. The US, too, needs to pay heed to the EU fiscal saga for at least two reasons. First, the weaknesses in the Eurozone will obviously strengthen the US dollar relative to the Euro; the resulting appreciation is likely to hurt US exports and thus its recovery, particularly in view of the continued failure of China to allow the Renminbi to adjust upwards. Second, like Greece, California too has had severe budgetary problems made worse by the large contractionary shock due to the US financial crisis. How will that eventually be resolved? With a bailout, and if so, from whom? While the global economy may have staved off the next great depression via massive fiscal stimuli, growing concerns about sovereign debt defaults dictate that governments start putting their public sector debt and deficits back on sustainable paths, without derailing the nascent global economic recovery.

# 10

# Banking Sector Internationalisation in Asia[1]

*(with Sasidaran Gopalan)*

Over the last decade, many emerging Asian economies have been liberalising their financial sectors, including opening up their banking systems to foreign competition. An immediate motivation for the adoption of this policy in countries such as Indonesia, South Korea and Thailand was the possible infusion of much-needed foreign funds that could help recapitalise their banks, following the Asian crisis of 1997–98. Apart from financing issues, however, it is becoming increasingly apparent that foreign competition tends to bring with it additional benefits that may not always result from domestic competition.

First, there is a growing body of empirical evidence of the benefits of foreign bank entry in emerging economies that come through reductions in cost structures, improvements in operational efficiency, the introduction and application of new technologies and banking products, marketing skills and management and corporate governance structures.[2] In addition, foreign banks could enhance the quality of human capital in the domestic banking system by importing high-skilled personnel to work in the local host subsidiary, which would also create knowledge spillovers to local employees. Customers should in turn benefit from access to new financial services.

Second, bank internationalisation may create domestic pressures for local banking authorities in the host countries to enhance and eventually harmonise regulatory and supervisory procedures and standards and overall financial infrastructure, working towards international best practice levels.

Third, entry of foreign banks ought to reduce the extent of "non-commercial" or "connected" lending as the incoming banks are not as politically connected like the home-grown institutions, and are therefore less susceptible to political patronage.

Fourth, opening up the domestic banking sector to foreign participation might encourage some local banks to venture overseas to compensate for loss of domestic revenue sources, or simply because they have learnt from the experiences of their foreign competitors who have entered the local market. For example, Singapore's domestic banking system has become more internationalised since 1997–98, and local banks in Singapore have not only consolidated their operations but also aggressively expanded their operations overseas, and have been active participants in cross-border mergers and takeovers. Singapore banks, for instance, have purchased significant stakes in banks in India, Hong Kong, Thailand, the Philippines and Indonesia, to name a few. Similarly, India's largest bank, the State Bank of India (SBI), has been aggressively establishing ventures overseas post 2000, just as the domestic market in India has become more open to foreign banks.

Fifth, a banking system with an internationally diversified asset base may be more stable and less crisis-prone. There is evidence, for instance, that foreign bank branches in South Korea, Malaysia and Thailand have lower non-performing loan (NPL) ratios than domestic banks. In addition, the domestic branches of foreign banks may be able to obtain financing from their foreign head office, which can act as a private lender of last resort during a period of financial stress. However, it is important to ensure that foreign investments do not mostly come from one home country, as this might increase rather than decrease instability. Diversification of exposure is the key to enhancing financial stability.[3]

Several Asian economies have witnessed crucial regulatory changes in their financial sectors since the Asian financial crisis. Most of the countries have come up with specific blueprints for restructuring their banking and financial sectors. While the details of these reforms obviously vary between countries, one of the central elements of all the restructuring plans has been the move to ease the entry norms for foreign banks, though the timing and pace has varied quite considerably. One of the key regulatory changes relating to foreign bank entry was the amendment of rules governing foreign equity limits in the domestic banking sector. These were dramatically altered post-crisis in some of the hard-hit countries. While countries such as Indonesia, South Korea and Thailand raised their foreign ownership limits quite aggressively, others, including China, India and Malaysia, took a more gradualist approach. But to what extent have these regulatory changes translated into tangible or *de facto* changes?

The evidence about the number and share of foreign banks in the domestic economy is somewhat unexpected, in that the number of foreign banks appears actually to have gone down in most of the countries (excluding the Philippines), despite the various regulations designed to ease entry norms for foreign banks (Table 10.1). However, this has largely been because of major consolidations and domestic restructurings among local banks. It is more worthwhile to examine the extent of market share of foreign banks in terms of assets and liabilities. Table 10.2

*Table 10.1* Number of foreign banks in emerging Asia

| Country | During the crisis (1997) | Post crisis (latest year available) |
|---|---|---|
| Indonesia | 44 | 37 (2005) |
| Malaysia | 14 | 13 (2008) |
| Thailand | 21 | 16 (2008) |
| Philippines | 13 | 22 (2008) |
| South Korea | 68 (1998) | 36 (2007) |
| China | N.A. | 71 (2007) |
| India | 42 | 29 (2007) |

*Notes*: In addition to branches and subsidiaries, "foreign banks" here include minority stakes, joint ventures, etc. Figures in parentheses denote the latest available year for that country. NA – Not Available.

*Source*: S. Gopalan and R. S. Rajan (2010). "Financial Sector De-regulation in Emerging Asia: Focus on Foreign Bank Entry", *The Journal of World Investment and Trade*, 11, pp.91–108.

*Table 10.2* Share of bank assets and deposits in emerging Asia by foreign banks with majority ownership

| | Share of banking assets (percentage) | | Share of banking deposits (percentage) | |
|---|---|---|---|---|
| **Countries** | **1997** | **2007–08** | **1997** | **2007–08** |
| Indonesia | 5.8 | 47 (2008) | 4.9 | 6.1 (2002) |
| Malaysia | 21.6 | 23 (2008) | 21.1 | 20.8 (2008) |
| Thailand | 7.1 | 12.6 (2008) | 2.9 | 7.8 (2008) |
| Philippines | 8.5 | 13.2 (2007) | N.A. | N.A. |
| South Korea | 2.2 | 15.7 (2008) | 3.8 | 10 (2002) |
| China | 0.1 | 2.3 (2007) | N.A. | N.A. |
| India | 7.9 | 8.4 (2008) | 7 | 5.8 (2008) |

*Note*: A bank is defined as foreign if it includes over 50 percent of shares. Figures in parentheses denote the latest available year for that country. N.A. – Not Available.

*Source*: S. Gopalan and R. S. Rajan (2010), *op. cit.*

therefore offers some indicative evidence on this by showing the extent of penetration by foreign banks with respect to their share of total assets and deposits.[4]

The levels of foreign bank penetration have increased dramatically not only in Indonesia and South Korea in particular, but also in Thailand and the Philippines, though to a somewhat lesser extent, especially in the case of foreign bank share of domestic assets. Not surprisingly, the penetration levels of foreign banks in China's domestic banking industry remained insignificant, with just 2.3 percent of total banking assets at the end of 2007, though this represents an increase from almost zero in 1997. India and Malaysia are interesting cases. As Table 10.2 indicates, there was no substantial change in the market share of foreign bank assets and deposits before and after the 1997 crisis in either of these countries; in fact the share of deposits of the foreign banks actually declined in both, if only marginally. This appears to be largely because of a rapid rise in the presence of private domestic commercial banks, which have taken the market share from national banks as well as foreign banks.

In Malaysia, the restrictions on foreign participation in its banking sector were largely maintained post-crisis. The share of foreign bank assets in Malaysia increased marginally from 21.6 percent in 1997 to about 23 percent in 2008, while the share of deposits remained stagnant. As Table 10.3 highlights, private domestic commercial banks controlled nearly 78 percent of the banking assets and deposits in Malaysia during the time of the crisis, and these aspects of the structure of the Malaysian banking system have remained broadly the same, even 10 years after the crisis. Given the overwhelming significance of the private domestic banks compared to foreign banks, mainly arising out of

*Table 10.3* Domestic private commercial bank assets and deposits in India and Malaysia

| | India | | Malaysia | |
|---|---|---|---|---|
| | **Share of banking assets (percent)** | **Share of banking deposits (percent)** | **Share of banking assets (percent)** | **Share of banking deposits (percent)** |
| 1997–98 | 10.1 | 8.3 | 78.8 | 78.1 |
| 2007–08 | 21.7[a] | 20.3[a] | 76.9 | 79.1 |

*Source*: [a] Compiled from Reserve Bank of India and Bank Negara Documents.

a favourable policy by the government to encourage domestic consolidation and privatisation, it has been difficult for the foreign banks to expand their presence in Malaysia.

While India's regulatory policies seem to provide an environment conducive to the entry and operation of foreign banks, the significance of foreign banks in the domestic banking industry has actually been declining since 1997, largely because of the rise in the private domestic banks. Specifically, the number of foreign banks operating in India has actually declined from 42 during 1997–98 to about 29 in 2007. While this was partly due to mergers between the Indian branches of foreign banks, there were also closures of some foreign banks in this period. As in Malaysia, domestic consolidations and privatisations were preferred to foreign bank entry per se. Thus, foreign bank assets made up nearly 8 percent of total commercial banking assets in 2007, almost on par with the levels during the 1997 financial crisis, while that of deposits declined from about 7 percent during 1997 to around 5.8 percent in 2008. On the other hand, as shown in Table 10.3, the significance of private sector banks has been growing steadily since 1997: they accounted for nearly 22 percent of all banking assets at the end of 2007, up from about 10 percent in 1997. The same trend holds for deposits: the share of deposits held by the private banks expanded significantly post-crisis from about 8 percent to 20 percent in 2007.

Overall, while Asian economies have been deregulating their banking systems for the reasons noted above, they have, as a group, approached this process somewhat more cautiously than their counterparts in East Europe and Latin America. Indeed, many Asian countries, especially China and India, are only at the early stages of internationalising their banking and financial systems. Part of this caution may be attributable to the continued presence of a strong anti-foreign bank lobby in some Asian countries. While some of the criticisms are misplaced and part of a larger "globophobia" phenomenon, there are some valid concerns with this policy.

There is a growing concern that foreign banks might be a source of instability and contagion rather than stability. This appears to have been the case in the global financial crisis of 2008–09 which hit the Eastern European financial system much harder than the more closed and regulated Asian financial system. Does foreign bank entry, or more broadly, internationalisation of the financial sector, make a country subject to international capital booms and reversals? Many casual observers of financial liberalisation fail to make a distinction between "capital account deregulation" (such as external borrowing), on the one hand, and "internationalisation of the financial sector", on the other.

The latter is broadly defined as the elimination of barriers to entry and discriminatory treatment of foreign competition, and cross-border provision of financial services. It is more likely that the capital account in the form of foreign bank lending makes a country more crisis-prone than when a foreign bank establishes a separate entity in the host country to lend domestically, especially in the form of a fully independent subsidiary (as opposed to a branch or representative office).[5]

Beyond this, the other broad economic justifications for continued protection of the domestic banking system boil down to the usual "infant industry" and "strategic" industry arguments. The first essentially argues that time is needed for domestic bank consolidation if local banks are to be able to compete effectively against multinational foreign banks which have much larger and more diversified capital bases. The second maintains that the financial sector, with its intricate linkages to the rest of the economy, is "too important to be left in the hands of foreigners".

While the infant industry argument has merit in theory, the usual problem in practice is that most infants take too long to grow up, and sometimes they grow old rather than grow up. The other problem with infant industries is that they become dependent on the state to protect them from threats, which tends to make them inefficient – and it is usually the consumer who loses out in the end. With regard to the strategic industry argument, one could turn it on its head and argue that given the importance of the banking and overall financial sector to the economy, everything possible must be done to ensure that it is as efficient as possible, which includes welcoming foreign bank participation. In any case, as with most other industries, the infant and strategic industry arguments appear more valid as grounds for moderating the pace, and possibly even the extent, of foreign bank entry, rather than opposing the policy in its entirety. From the regulators' perspective, any form of financial services liberalisation requires that the institutional and regulatory environment be fortified before and during the process of liberalisation. Liberalisation in a weak or ineffective regulatory and supervisory environment can be calamitous. This was made abundantly clear by the East Asian crisis of 1997–98, which was partly caused by the ill-timed and ill-sequenced liberalisation of the financial sector. This is an important reason for introducing competition in a phased and nuanced manner.

# Part III

# Asia and the Global Financial Architecture

# 11

# The Global Financial Crisis of 2008–2009: Implications for Emerging Asia[1]

The onset of the crisis in the US and Western Europe initially had only marginal impacts on emerging Asia. In the first instance there was an increase in gross outflows from Asian investors in 2008, as the initial response of some Asian investors – especially sovereign wealth funds (SWFs) – was to invest aggressively in selected US and European financial and related assets, believing them to be grossly under-priced. However, as the crisis intensified, and with the prospect of being faced with significant capital losses with the collapse of major financial institutions and overall asset prices in the developed world, these gross outflows from Asia probably tapered off, if they were not reversed completely.

While there were increasing fears about the impact of the crisis on the overall US economy, the catch-word in Asia in 2007–08 was "decoupling". As long as the slowdown in the US was not "too sharp", the belief was that the rapid growth in China and India as well as the revitalisation of the Japanese economy would at least cushion the region, if not completely offset the slowdown in the US, and ensure that the region's growth momentum was not completely derailed. In fact, in 2009, the Asian Development Bank (ADB) in its flagship publication, *Asian Development Outlook*, referred to "Asia's relative immunity" from the crisis due to "only limited exposure to sub-prime and related products...".[2] This relative optimism was also mirrored in the initial IMF forecasts of mid-2008 for regional growth in 2009–2010.[3] Regional equity prices, too, remained fairly robust until early 2008. While a slowdown from 2008 levels was widely anticipated, it was expected to be relatively mild, and things appeared relatively manageable for the region as a whole until summer 2008, after which credit markets worldwide froze and emerging market spreads widened markedly.

The heightened risk aversion worldwide – particularly following the collapse of Lehman Brothers in September 2008 – led to an abrupt about-turn in gross capital inflows from all emerging economies (see Chapter 1). This turnaround in capital flows then led to broad-based asset price declines and moderate exchange rate depreciations, which would have been even larger if not for some degree of foreign exchange intervention (Figures 11.1 and 11.2). While exchange rate depreciations were most apparent in the case of countries with current account deficits, namely South Korea, India and Indonesia, even countries with current account surpluses, such as Singapore and Malaysia, experienced exchange rate pressure, as is apparent from the drop in their reserves. Interestingly, China and Hong Kong were exceptions to this trend, both economies continuing to accumulate reserves even during the height of the financial crisis.

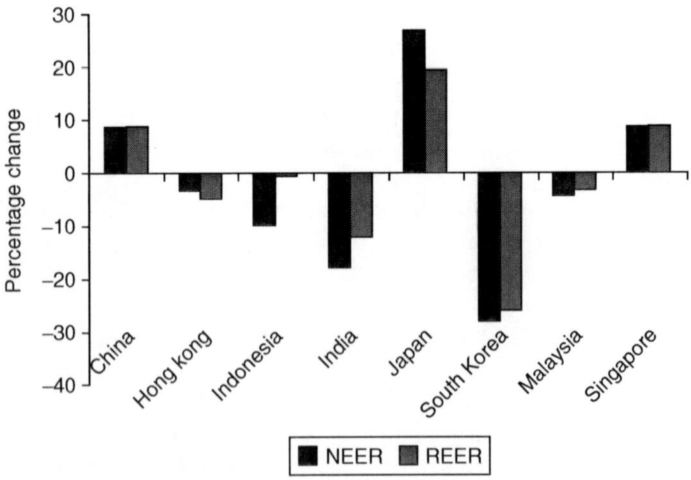


*Figure 11.1* Nominal and real effective exchange rate changes in selected emerging Asian economies, 2007–09 (percentage; between August 2007 and September 2009)

*Notes*: A negative (positive) change implies depreciation (appreciation). The effective exchange rate is the weighted average of 58 trading partners reported by the BIS.

*Source*: Bank for International Settlements.

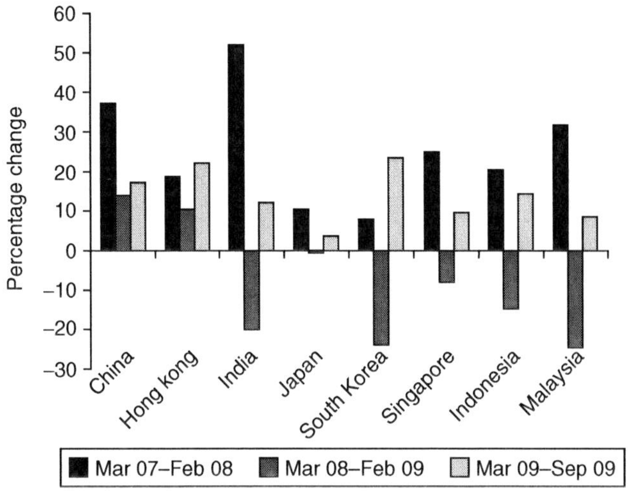


*Figure 11.2* Change in international reserves of selected emerging Asian economies, 2007–09 (percentage)

*Source*: Author's computations from CEIC database.

Countries in Asia were also particularly badly impacted because of the sharp decline in trade financing, much of which involved US dollars (regional trade being largely invoiced in US dollars). There was a synchronised economic slump, including in Japan, where production and exports contracted quite sharply in the fourth quarter of 2009, mainly due to the decline in global demand for cars, IT and capital goods. The impact of this shock on Asia was apparent from the sudden drop-off in Chinese exports in late 2009 and the resulting decline in exports of the rest of Asia to China, as well as more generally. There was a spike in inventory-to-shipment ratios, as firms in Asia were not able to get the financing necessary to buy or sell their goods. It is worth noting that the collapse in Asian exports was much worse than during the Asian crisis a decade ago. Thus a notable consequence of this double whammy – an alarming contraction in trade and capital flows – was that the Asian region witnessed a very sharp contraction in industrial production.[4]

Table 11.1 offers a summary comparison of the sizeable declines in economic growth in various regions of the world during the crisis period (2007–09).[5] The deterioration in growth rates witnessed in emerging Asia was quite significant: the average growth rate decline for

*Table 11.1* Economic growth slowdown in emerging Asia and elsewhere, 2007–09 (percentage)

| Country group name | 2007 | 2008 | 2009[a] | 2009–2007 (difference) |
|---|---|---|---|---|
| Emerging Asia[b] | 7.4 | 4.5 | −1.3 | −8.6 |
| Developing Asia[c] | 10.6 | 7.7 | 5.5 | −5.1 |
| ASEAN-5[d] | 6.3 | 4.9 | −0.3 | −6.6 |
| South Asia[e] | 8.6 | 6.3 | 5.6[f] | −3.0 |
| (NIEs) Newly industrialised Asian economies[f] | 5.7 | 1.6 | −5.2 | −10.9 |
| Central and Eastern Europe | 5.4 | 2.9 | −5.0 | −10.4 |
| CIS and Mongolia | 8.6 | 5.5 | −5.8 | −14.4 |
| Middle East | 6.3 | 5.9 | 2.0 | −4.3 |
| Western hemisphere | 5.7 | 4.2 | −2.6 | −8.3 |
| Memo: | | | | |
| World | 5.2 | 3.2 | −1.4 | −6.6 |
| Advanced economies | 2.7 | 0.9 | −3.8 | −6.5 |
| Emerging and developing economies | 8.3 | 6.1 | 1.5 | −6.8 |

*Notes*: [a]Forecast for 2009, as of July 2009. [b]Emerging Asia: China, Hong Kong, India, Indonesia, Malaysia, Singapore, South Korea, Thailand. [c]Developing Asia: Bangladesh, Bhutan, Cambodia, China, Fiji, India, Indonesia, Kiribati, Lao PDR, Maldives, Myanmar, Nepal, Pakistan, Papua New Guinea, Philippines, Samoa, Solomon Islands, Sri Lanka, Thailand, Tonga, Vanuatu, Vietnam. [d]ASEAN-5: Indonesia, Malaysia, Philippines, Thailand, Vietnam. [e]South Asia: Afghanistan, Bangladesh, Bhutan, India, Maldives, Nepal, Pakistan and Sri Lanka. [f]NIEs – Hong Kong, Singapore, South Korea, Taiwan Province of China.

*Sources*: Adapted from M. Goldstein and D. Xie (2009. "The Impact of the Financial Crisis on Emerging Asia", Proceedings, Federal Reserve Bank of San Francisco, pp.27–80 and Asian Development Bank (ADB) (2009). *Asian Development Outlook 2009*, ADB.

the region during this period was 8.6 percentage points. The decline in growth rates has been much more severe in East and Southeast Asia (6.6 and 10.9 percentage points, respectively) compared to the somewhat less open South Asian economies (3 percentage points decline).

After the sharp downturn in the latter part of 2008 and early 2009, the global and Asian economies appear to have stabilised; much of Asia experienced a sharper than expected rebound, largely due to "a return to normalcy following the abrupt collapse of global trade and finance at the end of 2008. Just as the US downturn triggered an outsized fall in Asia's GDP because international trade froze...trade normalization [has been]...generating an outsized Asian upturn...".[6] In addition, there was a discernible thawing of credit markets and return of an appetite for risk. Timely and aggressive liquidity support, as well as the large fiscal stimuli in several countries in the region, was also an extremely important driver of recovery in Asia. The largely liquidity-induced surges in the global stock markets (albeit from a low base) have also undoubtedly added to the momentum of the recovery (though the sustainability of the market run-up remains to be seen), as have the relative easing of commodity prices.

Most observers, including the IMF, underestimated the potential impact of the global financial crisis on Asia, and the sharp turnaround that followed. The region's large international reserve holdings, the lower levels of leverage especially with regard to external short-term foreign currency debt in the region, along with stronger balance sheets of Asian corporates and financial institutions, have worked together to ensure the capital account shock will not have long-lasting effects on Asia this time, unlike in 1997–98.[7] The painful structural changes that the region has gone through since the 1997–98 crisis, as well as the more cautious approach towards capital account liberalisation and foreign bank entry in a number of these economies, helped to mitigate the extent of damage they suffered in the global financial crisis of 2008–09.

The medium-term challenge for emerging Asia, if it hopes to return to a period of sustained robust growth, must be to place a greater emphasis on generating domestic and regional demand. Among other things, this would require a reconfiguration of real exchange rates towards the production and consumption of nontradables, as well as a focus on recycling current account surpluses intraregionally (see Chapter 5).

# 12

# Sequencing of Regional Cooperation in Asia: The Real and Financial Dimensions

While "Asian economic cooperation and integration" has been a long-standing topic of debate in intellectual and policy arenas, there has been a particular heightening of interest in the subject over the last few years. This is for a number of reasons:[1]

i) The contagious effects of the Asian economic crisis of 1997–98, along with the perceived inadequate responses to the crisis by multilateral agencies and extra-regional economic powers such as the US and the EU.
ii) Some notable external developments in regionalism, including moves to create a Free Trade Area of the Americas (FTAAs), and more importantly, the enlargement of the EU and the successful launch of the Euro.
iii) The rapid and sustained growth in, and consequent economic emergence of, China and India, and the realisation that these two emerging Asian giants have been altering the dynamics of the global economy and will continue to do so for some time to come.
iv) The global financial crisis (GFC) and expected continued slowdown in the developed Western world, which has reinforced concerns in Asia about "over dependence" on extra-regional export markets.

Despite the attention paid to the issue of Asian economic cooperation and integration, one fundamental question has remained unanswered – what does one mean by economic cooperation and integration (broadly referred to as "economic regionalism" in this chapter)?[2] It is important to distinguish between three broad forms of economic regionalism: trade, financial and monetary. Since the Asian crisis of 1997–98, Asian countries have made some progress in all three areas.[3] This chapter explores the conceptual definitions of economic cooperation and integration in the financial, monetary and trade spheres.

In the area of trade cooperation, there has been a proliferation of free trade agreements (FTAs), involving many Asian countries. These FTAs have gone well beyond just liberalisation of trade in goods, encompassing liberalisation of trade in services and other behind-the-border measures which lead to "deep integration" among partners. These measures include investment protection and the liberalisation, harmonisation and mutual recognition of standards and certification, protection of intellectual property rights (IPRs), opening of government procurement markets, streamlining and harmonisation of customs procedures, and development of dispute settlement procedures.[4]

In the areas of finance, while the regional economies are taking noteworthy steps to strengthen, upgrade and integrate their financial systems, the contagious nature of the 1997–98 crisis has led many observers and policymakers to the view that there are positive externalities from cooperating to strengthen their individual financial sectors, develop regional financial markets, and diversify their financial structures away from bank-based systems to bond markets. In this regard two main initiatives are underway in East Asia. One is the Asian Bond Fund (ABF), established by the eleven members of the Executives' Meeting of East Asia-Pacific Central Banks (EMEAP),[5] and the other is the Asian Bond Market Initiative (ABMI) by ASEAN Plus Three (APT) economies.[6] The latter, endorsed at the APT Finance Ministers Meeting in Manila in August 2003, focuses primarily on developing efficient bond markets in Asia to enable the private and public sectors to raise and invest long-term capital. The activities of the ABMI are primarily concentrated on facilitating access to the market through a wider variety of issuers and enhancing market infrastructure to foster bond markets in Asia.

The Asian Bond Fund (ABF) was established on June 2, 2003. The first stage of the ABF essentially involved the regional governments voluntarily contributing about 1 percent each of their reserves to a fund dedicated to purchasing regional sovereign and semi-sovereign bonds denominated in US dollars. The initial size of the ABF was about USD 1 billion and the fund has been passively managed by the investment management unit of the Swiss-based Bank for International Settlements (BIS). The mandate has been to invest in bonds in eight of the eleven member countries of EMEAP, the developed countries of Australia, New Zealand and Japan being the sole lenders to the ABF. In a noteworthy next step, the ABF 2 (second stage of the ABF) was established in December 2004. The size of the fund was doubled (USD 2 billion), and its mandate was to invest in selected domestic currency sovereign and quasi-sovereign bonds in the eight countries.

In broad terms, the objectives of the ABF are four-fold. First, to diversify debt financing from bank lending to bond financing by developing regional financial/capital markets by reducing supply-side constraints and introducing low-cost products and raising investor awareness and broadening investor base on the demand side. Second, to encourage a convergence in the financial and capital market policies and accelerate improvements in financial market infrastructure. Third, to recycle regional funds intraregionally and also reduce the region's vulnerability to "fickle" international investors. Fourth, to reduce the extent of currency and maturity mismatches (i.e. "double mismatches").[7]

Beyond the ABF, more intensive financial cooperation would involve agreeing to regional financial standards and prudential measures, cross-trading of financial instruments in various national markets and facilitating intraregional payments and settlements (also see Chapter 14 on the Asian Currency Unit).

In the case of monetary regionalism there are various gradations of policy measures. In Asia, two recent monetary initiatives have involved steps to enhance regional financial surveillance and policy dialogue (the weakest form of monetary regionalism), as well as the Chiang-Mai initiative (CMI), a series of bilateral swap and repurchase agreements among the APT countries. There has also been some discussion about the possibility of pooling part of the region's international reserves as a means of safeguarding against financial crisis (see Chapter 13). More intensive forms of monetary regionalism range from exchange rate coordination (including regional basket pegs or a regionally-harmonised exchange rate band) to full monetary integration with a single currency and common monetary policy.

The links between trade and financial regionalism are fairly straightforward. Efforts to facilitate trade and financial flows are largely complementary and can be undertaken simultaneously. For instance, financial integration will presumably make it easier for a country to obtain the financing needed to grease the wheels of trade.[8] Availability of financing will also promote cross-border investments, hence facilitating trade integration (as much of trade occurs following FDI).[9] For instance, it is generally recognised that cross-border trade financing is a crucial determinant of trade flows. Similarly, FDI flows require complementary project financing.[10] Conversely, trade integration may lead to greater synchronisation of business cycles (discussed below), which in turn lead to similar interest rate movements, i.e. *de facto* financial integration. For instance, studies have found bilateral trade flows to be an important determinant of cross-country financial linkages.[11] In terms of actual sequencing, trade and the weaker forms of financial cooperation can be undertaken simultaneously, while stronger forms of financial cooperation, such as the integration of institutional structures and harmonisation of standards should come later.[12]

Less clear are the links between trade and finance regionalism, on the one hand, and monetary regionalism, on the other. The economic case for or against monetary integration is typically based on the optimum currency area (OCA) criterion, which weighs the microeconomic benefits of a common currency (lower transactions costs, ability to economise on reserve holdings, reduction in regional price discrimination and elimination of other costs of interregional exchange rate uncertainty) against the costs of forsaking exchange rate adjustments as a policy instrument and loss of monetary policy autonomy. The criteria for ascertaining the feasibility of a common or optimum currency area (OCA) have focused on the degree of factor mobility between partners, size and openness, trade diversification, dissimilarity of commodity composition of production and trade baskets, macroeconomic trends and the synchronisation of business cycles, the degree of labour market flexibility, and the scope for regional transfers of potential members.[13]

*Does deeper financial integration imply that a region is closer to or further away from being an OCA?* At a basic level, financial integration implies an enhanced degree of capital mobility and a consequent loss of monetary policy autonomy. This being the case, the next step to creating a common regional currency may not be very costly and could offer participants a number of microeconomic benefits. In addition, as pointed out early on by Nobel Laureate Robert Mundell, agents in countries with open capital accounts can adjust their portfolio wealth holdings in response to country-specific shocks (by borrowing or lending/investing abroad) or can cushion themselves from idiosyncratic shocks by drawing on income from foreign asset holdings (rentals, dividends etc).[14] To the extent that this portfolio adjustment or income insurance mechanism reduces the need for exchange rate adjustments in the event of asymmetric shocks (shocks that affect members of a union disproportionately), financial integration could help the region go some way towards satisfying the OCA criteria.

*Does deeper trade integration imply that a region is closer or farther away from being an OCA?* On the one hand, greater trade integration leads to a convergence of aggregate demand patterns in the trade partners, making them more likely to have common business cycles and rendering unilateral exchange rate adjustments relatively ineffective as an expenditure switching tool.[15] On the other hand, if intraregional trade is dominated by industrial specialisation and inter-industry trade, or intra-industry trade (IIT) involving vertical specialisation, the countries' production structures may actually become more dissimilar and thus more vulnerable to asymmetric supply shocks. This in turn could weaken the case for monetary integration, since independent monetary tools or a flexible exchange rate may be needed to compensate for asymmetrical shocks.[16] It is therefore an empirical issue as to which of these effects – supply (asymmetry) or demand (symmetry) – will dominate.

According to one study that used a sample of annual data for 147 countries over the period 1960–99, the impact of trade integration between industrial country pairs on output fluctuations is 0.092, significantly higher than the impact between developing country pairs (0.019) or between industrial and developing country pairs (0.037).[17] The authors of the study conjectured that this may be due to higher IIT between industrial countries compared to inter-industry trade involving developing countries. More specific evidence to date for selected Asian economies suggests that the volume of intra-Asian trade does not necessarily lead to more symmetrical business cycles and could actually cause more idiosyncratic business cycles.[18]

There is a growing body of literature which suggests that the tendency towards specialisation in production could be strengthened as financial integration permits the diversification or sharing of risks internationally (i.e. insurance via financial markets), hence allowing firms to locate production in one country and benefit from scale economies (or market size effects and linkages), thick labour markets and pure external economies.[19] This consequent lower degree of industrial diversification in turn makes countries more susceptible to idiosyncratic shocks and therefore less likely to satisfy OCA criteria. Thus, even while financial integration may exacerbate supply-side asymmetries between members, synchronisation of business cycles may not be a pre-requisite for sharing a common currency if agents could insure themselves in international financial markets. Indeed, from the perspective of international risk sharing it would be preferable if member economies' financial market returns were not synchronised.[20]

While the preceding discussion asked whether financial-cum-trade integration makes a common regional currency more feasible, some have suggested the reverse causation. By reducing transactions and information costs, a single currency may itself facilitate trade and financial flows amongst members. There is a large and growing body of evidence based on gravity models using both cross-sectional and time series data that suggests that a common currency stimulates trade.[21] Similarly, and less controversially, it is generally recognised that elimination of the costs that invariably exist with segmented domestic financial markets, as well as convergence in macro-policies and micro-prudential statutes and regulations, will deepen and broaden regional financial markets and lessen the degree of intraregional financial segmentation. Proponents of European integration used such an argument extensively to justify the region's Economic and Monetary Union and they seem to have been proved correct, at least in the case of the financial markets.[22] In other words, OCA criteria may be endogenous, i.e., the structure of the economy is endogenous to economic policy.[23]

It is plausible that a regional trade-cum-financial arrangement may be undermined by lack of macroeconomic coordination and exchange rate instability amongst members. Specifically, competitive devaluations may generate a protectionist backlash, which goes against the purpose of the regional trade-cum-financial arrangement and may even threaten its existence, as the experience of Mercosur (FTA of Argentina, Brazil, Paraguay and Uruguay) suggests. The devaluation of the Brazilian real in 1999 accentuated the overvaluation of the Argentine peso and contributed to the economic crisis in Argentina, which in turn had significant negative repercussions on the Uruguayan banking system. Trade partners were effectively pursuing competitive exchange rate policies. More generally, evidence based on thirty seven countries and six regional FTAs suggests that the adverse effects of uncoordinated exchange rate policy may be more pronounced within the context of a regional trade arrangement.[24] These adverse effects can be expected to be greater the deeper the real sector integration, as the cross-price elasticity of demand for similar goods and services produced within the integrated region may rise ("knife-edge" comparative advantage). It is in this context, Barry Eichengreen has noted:[25]

> The irony is that an FTA designed to foster better commercial relations between Argentina and Brazil has in fact seen a heightening of trade tensions between them, due largely to instability in currency markets. (p.2)

What should Asia do in the future to promote economic cooperation and integration? There is a complex set of causal interconnections between financial, trade and monetary integration. While monetary integration may give rise to some self-validating processes that may facilitate trade-cum-financial integration, deeper integration is unlikely to occur dynamically following monetary integration. Given the divergences in economic and institutional structures in the region and the lack of genuine political commitment, any attempt to create a full-fledged Asian Monetary Union (AMU) is very premature.[26] Asia's focus should instead continue to be on enhancing trade-cum-financial cooperation by reducing distortions and barriers to cross-border economic activity.

There appears to be more scope for systematic cooperation on a region-wide basis in the financial arena. Regional governments should persist with attempts to develop well-functioning financial markets and institutions. Particular attention needs to be paid to deepening and upgrading national and regional government and corporate bond markets as a means of reducing the region's heavy reliance on banks. While the Asian Bond Funds (I and II) are modest steps in the right direction, an interesting suggestion in this regard is to set up an Asian Bond Corporation (ABC) aimed at creating and issuing basket currency bonds (weighted combinations of regional currencies of the underlying national bonds) backed by regional sovereign bonds.[27] Conceptually, the ABC appears to be a particularly innovative proposal, and if successful, could (a) facilitate the development of regional bond markets; (b) reduce the extent of currency mismatch; and (c) provide a fillip for the eventual creation of an Asian Currency Unit (ACU) (see Chapter 14).

However, we conclude with the usual – but never irrelevant – caveats. First, the devil lies in the detail, and poor implementation could kill even the best thought-out proposal. Second, any proposal to establish a regional institution must take into account the transaction costs of setting up such a scheme. Third, while the successful implementation of these financial market initiatives ought to bolster the extent of regional financial integration, it is critical that they do not detract from domestic structural reforms to broaden and deepen individual capital markets. After all, a regional alliance is only as strong as its weakest link.

# 13
# Revisiting Asian Monetary and Financial Cooperation

An important lesson that the Asian economies took away from the Asian financial crisis of 1997–98 was the need to accumulate reserves as a safeguard against future financial crises. Reserve build-up in the region has been phenomenal (admittedly, some of it has been due to exchange rate policies per se). Interestingly, many chose not to allow their reserves to decline too rapidly during the global financial crisis (GFC) of 2008–09, realising that the use of reserves is not always effective during all crises.[1] So, after the GFC, the region has again been stockpiling reserves (Figure 13.1). However, the crisis has made these countries face up to the fact that there are limits to own reserve accumulation as a means of self-insurance. Specifically, since the opportunity costs can get prohibitively high how much is enough?

Against this background, and in recognition that financial stability has the characteristics of a regional public good, it is understandable that Asian countries have been eager to promote regional monetary cooperation. The Chiang-Mai Initiative (CMI) has taken centre stage in this regard. The initiative has so far consisted of a series of bilateral swap arrangements between the ASEAN Plus Three (APT) economies (i.e. ASEAN plus China, Japan and South Korea) (Table 13.1).

As far back as the 8th Asean Plus Three (APT) Finance Ministers' Meeting in Istanbul in May 2005 there was an agreement to re-evaluate the process, including the possibility of regionalising the arrangements. As part of this there was an agreement to explore the feasibility of developing a collective mechanism to activate the swaps. There was also a recognition of the need to increase the extent of regional dialogue and surveillance and link these more closely and effectively to the CMI.[2] There was not much progress on these issues until recently. However, at the April 2009 meeting of APT Finance Ministers in Phuket, Thailand,

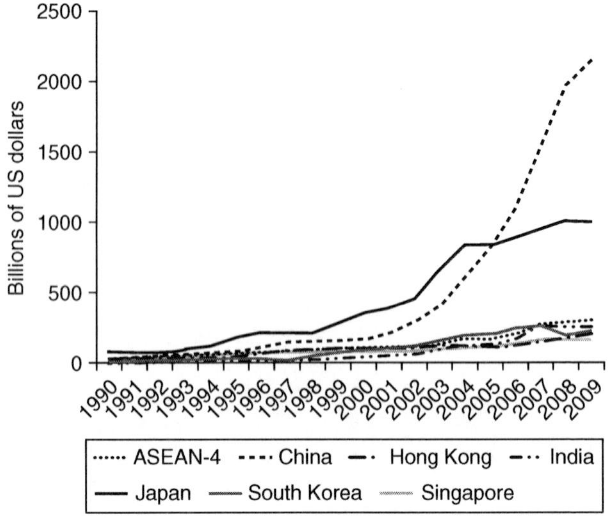


*Figure 13.1* International reserve holdings by emerging Asia, 1990–2009*
**Note*: 2009 (July).
*Source*: Author's computations from CEIC database.

the APT countries finally reached an agreement to transform the existing bilateral arrangements into a regional foreign reserve pool of USD 120 billion to address short-term liquidity constraints in the region and to supplement the existing international financial arrangements.

The CMI multilateralisation (CMIM) is essentially a first step in creating a regional reserve pool (Table 13.2). The "Plus Three" countries of China, Japan and South Korea will contribute 80 percent, with the ten ASEAN countries' sharing the remaining 20 percent. Of this, Japan will contribute USD 38.4 billion to the pool (it has also separately extended USD 60 billion of Yen-denominated swap facilities), as will China (in conjunction with Hong Kong), while South Korea will contribute USD 19.2 billion. Within ASEAN the contributions of member economies will be made primarily by Indonesia, Malaysia, Thailand and Singapore (each contributing USD 4.76 billion) and the Philippines (USD 3.68 billion). The CMIM is consistent with suggestions made previously that the region should create a reserve pool with three tiers of liquidity. The first tier is owned reserves, which offers the highest degree of liquidity and has zero conditionality, but is costly. The second tier is subdivided into a country's own reserves placed with the regional pool and

*Table 13.1* Network of bilateral swap arrangements (BSAs) under the Chiang-Mai Initiative (CMI)*

Total: USD 90 Billion[a] ASEAN swap arrangement USD 2 billion (As of April 2009)

| | **Japan** | **China** | **Korea** | **Thailand** | **Brunei** | **Malaysia** | **Cambodia** | **Philippines** | **Lao PDR** | **Myanmar** | **Indonesia** | **Vietnam** | **Singapore** |
|---|---|---|---|---|---|---|---|---|---|---|---|---|---|
| Japan | | Eq. 3[b] | 10 / Eq.3[c,d] | 6 | | 1 | | 6 | | | 12 | | 3 |
| China | Eq. 3[b] | | Eq. 4[e] | 2 | | 1.5 | | Eq.2[f] | | | 4 | | |
| Korea | 5/ Eq.3 | Eq. 4[e] | | 1 | | 1.5 | | 2 | | | 2 | | |
| Thailand | 3 | | 1 | | | | | | | | | | |
| Brunei | | | | | | | | | | | | | |
| Malaysia | | | 1.5 | | | | | | | | | | |
| Cambodia | | | | | | | | | | | | | |
| Philippines | 0.5 | | 2 | | | | | | | | | | |
| Lao PDR | | | | | | | | | | | | | |
| Myanmar | | | | | | | | | | | | | |
| Indonesia | | | 2 | | | | | | | | | | |
| Vietnam | | | | | | | | | | | | | |
| Singapore | 1 | | | | | | | | | | | | |

*Notes*: * In USD billions (or equivalent). [a]The sum of USD 90 billion does not include the USD 2 billion of the ASEAN Swap Arrangement (ASA) (as of April 2009). [b]Local Currency Swap between Japanese YEN and Chinese YUAN. [c]Local Currency Swap between Japanese YEN and Korean WON. [d]The maximum amount is increased to USD 20 billion equivalent until the end of October 2009. [e]Local Currency Swap between Chinese YUAN and Korean WON. [f]Local Currency Swap between Chinese YUAN and Philippine PESO.

*Source*: www.mof.go.jp/english/if/CMI_0904.pdf

*Table 13.2* CMIM contributions and purchasing multiples

| | Financial contribution | | | | Purchasing multiple |
|---|---|---|---|---|---|
| | USD (billion) | | (percent) | | |
| China | 38.40 | China (*Exc. Hong Kong*) 34.20 | 32.00 | 28.50 | 0.5 |
| | | Hong Kong, 4.20 | | 3.50 | 2.5 |
| Japan | 38.40 | | 32.00 | | 0.5 |
| South Korea | 19.20 | | 16.00 | | 1 |
| **Plus 3** | **96.00** | | **80.00** | | – |
| Indonesia | 4.77 | | 3.97 | | 2.5 |
| Thailand | 4.77 | | 3.97 | | 2.5 |
| Malaysia | 4.77 | | 3.97 | | 2.5 |
| Singapore | 4.77 | | 3.97 | | 2.5 |
| Philippines | 3.68 | | 3.07 | | 2.5 |
| Vietnam | 1.00 | | 0.83 | | 5 |
| Cambodia | 0.12 | | 0.10 | | 5 |
| Myanmar | 0.06 | | 0.05 | | 5 |
| Brunei | 0.03 | | 0.02 | | 5 |
| Lao PDR | 0.03 | | 0.02 | | 5 |
| **ASEAN** | 24.00 | | 20.00 | | – |
| **Total** | 120.00 | | 100.00 | | – |

*Notes*: *Hong Kong, China's purchasing is limited to the IMF de-linked portion because Hong Kong, China is not a member of the IMF.

*Source*: Reproduced from www.mof.go.jp/english/if/100324press_release.pdf

other members' reserves with the pool. The third tier is conventional IMF lending. With such a structure, the degree of liquidity could be inversely related to the degree of conditionality.[3] While this is a longer-term goal, tellingly, the regional monetary arrangement was not called upon during the global financial crisis. Instead, some countries, such as South Korea, which needed US dollar liquidity availed themselves of bilateral swaps with the US Federal Reserve (Table 13.3).

Clearly there are problems with the regional arrangement. Among the things that need to be rethought is the existing criterion that the cumulative CMIM drawing by any country that exceeds 20 percent of a country's quota must involve IMF conditionality. Such IMF conditionality is unlikely to be acceptable to most East Asian policymakers,

*Table 13.3* Swap lines opened with Central Banks

| Date | Central Bank |
|---|---|
| December 12, 2007 | European Central Bank, Swiss National Bank. |
| September 18, 2008 | Bank of Japan, Bank of England, Bank of Canada. |
| September 24, 2008 | Reserve Bank of Australia, Sveriges Riksbank, Norges Bank, Danmarks Nationalbank. |
| October 28, 2008 | Reserve Bank of New Zealand. |
| October 29, 2008 | Banco Central do Brasil, Banco de México, Bank of Korea, Monetary Authority of Singapore. |

*Source*: M. J. Fleming and N. J. Klagge (2010). "The Federal Reserve's Foreign Exchange Swap Lines", *Current Issues*, 16, FRBNY.

given the painful memories of the Asian financial crisis. Of course, greater independence from the IMF in turn requires that the APT take a much bigger part in enhancing the quality of intraregional economic surveillance mechanisms (including more rigorous and transparent peer review) and devising a set of conditionalities to guide decisions on regional liquidity provisions.[4]

Thus, the announcement of strengthening of surveillance alongside the creating of the CMIM is an important step.[5] Note, however, that surveillance itself is insufficient if it lacks teeth and if it does not include remedial actions by regional members found to be running unsustainable policies. There is also the equally difficult problem of what such a regional liquidity arrangement implies for exchange rate coordination. Countries with relatively fixed exchange rates will require rather more reserves to manage their currencies and/or pursue much more disciplined domestic economic policies, while countries running more flexible regimes could cause or be faced with competitiveness pressures in the near-term vis-à-vis the other countries if their currencies appreciate or depreciate sharply. Neither surveillance nor exchange rate coordination is issues that have seen much progress in Asia to date, leaving one somewhat sceptical about how viable or effective the CMIM, or any sort of regional liquidity arrangement, might be in the future.

# 14
# The Idea and Reality of the Asian Currency Unit (ACU)[1]

There has been much talk about whether Asia is decoupling from the US. Will Asia be able to withstand a sharp downturn in the US economy? As of now the answer must surely be "no". The region is heavily dependent on the US and the European Union (EU) as the final destinations for its exports. There are also many other intricate monetary and financial linkages between the US and Asia, including the heavy dependence of the region on US dollar-denominated assets. However, as Asia continues on its path of intensified economic monetary and financial regionalism (MFR), it is conceivable that the region can become more independent from the US. It is in this context that one needs to understand recent events in Asian MFR.

There are many degrees of MFR, ranging from the weak form, involving regional policy dialogue and surveillance, on the one hand, to exchange rate and monetary coordination, on the other. East Asian economies have made notable strides in promoting policy dialogue. For instance, the Economic Review and Policy Dialogue (ERPD) was established in 2000 to exchange information, conduct regional surveillance and use peer pressure for enhancing national and regional policies. The regional economies have also taken a number of steps to enhance "medium" forms of MFR, broadly defined as the development of regional liquidity arrangements and regional financial markets.

In the monetary realm, the most notable medium form of MFR in Asia has been the Chiang-Mai Initiative or CMI (see Chapter 13). In the financial area, the two main initiatives under way are the Asian Bond Fund (ABF), established by the eleven members of the Executives' Meeting of East Asia-Pacific Central Bank (EMEAP), and the Asian Bond Market Initiative (ABMI), set up by the ASEAN plus Three (APT) economies. While most observers concur that the time is not ripe for Asia to consider a common currency in the near future, there has been some discussion about the possible creation of an Asian Currency Unit (ACU) as a means of deepening monetary integration.

The ACU is a weighted average of regional currencies in the style of the European Currency Unit (ECU), which was created in 1979 under the European Monetary System (EMS) and remained in operation until the launch of the Euro in 1999. There are in fact at least three rationales for an ACU: as a unit of account, as a divergence indicator and for exchange rate stabilisation.[2]

*a) Unit of account*: At the micro level the rationale for an ACU is to enable regional economic agents to invoice regional financial and trade transactions in the ACU, reducing the region's dependence on the US dollar and other external currencies. The ACU could also be used to devise new instruments that can be easily traded across borders without an underlying exchange rate risk. Importers and exporters could denominate intra-Asia trade in ACUs. Asian governments or corporates might wish to issue sovereign or corporate bonds in ACUs. The various central banks could hold part of their reserves in ACUs and even commercial banks could take deposits and give loans denominated in ACUs. If successful, intraregional intermediation of savings might be promoted, in the process possibly reducing the region's exposure to external shocks.

However, in reality, it is unlikely that the ACU, even if it does come into existence, will be used on a widespread basis for some time to come. The experience of Europe is instructive in this regard. The initial creation of the ECU did not lead to a widespread use of the unit. Even in the 1990s, until the actual creation of the Euro, the vast majority of intra-European financial and trade transactions were not in ECUs but primarily in US dollars and other sovereign national European currencies. So it is not just the creation of a currency unit that is important; there has to be coordinated agreement by regional bodies to start transacting in the new unit, failing which no one will want to take the first step. This inertial effect of existing currencies (the advantage of incumbency) is based on the concept of "network externalities" or "lock-in" effects, whereby there are limited incentives for economic agents to unilaterally take on a new currency (particularly for invoicing transactions).

*b) Divergence indicator*: The ADB has suggested that in its initial stages the ACU should serve mainly as a means of benchmarking the extent of currency movements/deviations, i.e. as a divergence indicator. As the ADB president Haruhiko Kuroda noted, "The ACU ... could be used to monitor the stability of participating currencies and would tangibly demonstrate the need for greater exchange rate coordination. What Asia needs here is basically an exchange rate that is flexible toward the rest of the world but relatively stable within the region."[3] In effect, the ACU, as a regional benchmark, can act as a tool for monitoring foreign exchange market conditions; it could help explain the degree of divergence of each participating country's currencies, which help us understand the idiosyncratic problems in a particular currency's market, and in pursuing appropriate macroeconomic policies.

*c) Exchange rate stabilisation*: It has also been suggested that the ACU could be used as a means of enhancing *internal* exchange rate stability if the regional central banks were to stabilise their respective currencies to the regional unit (thereby helping to reduce the risk of regional competitive devaluations). The notion of stabilisation vis-à-vis an internal basket in the manner of Europe's Exchange Rate Mechanism (ERM) is distinct from stabilisation vis-à-vis an external unit, which would require that the ACU in turn be pegged in some way to an external currency such as the US dollar or Euro, or some weighted average thereof.

Focusing on the notion of stabilisation vis-à-vis an internal basket (i.e. regional currencies benchmarking movements to the ACU), while the potential microeconomic benefits noted above do not require internal stabilisation, such stabilisation could promote the more widespread use of the ACU. This is because the regional central banks will automatically begin to use the ACU more extensively as a reserve, and possibly even as an intervention currency, thus providing an additional inducement for private agents to make greater use of the unit in invoicing and transactions. Nonetheless, given the divergences in economic and institutional structures in the region, and in the absence of macroeconomic policy coordination and mechanisms for automatic intraregional fiscal transfers, any attempt at formal exchange rate coordination – including internal stabilisation vis-à-vis the ACU – is far too risky and premature and is likely to be a failure, setting back the prospects for other forms of economic integration.

One feasible way forward for Asia might be for the region to establish an ACU as a parallel currency, with regional economies free to choose among themselves if and to what extent they want to manage their respective currencies against the ACU as well as external currencies such as the US dollar and the Euro. It is important to keep in mind that management does not involve pegging. One could, for instance, think of a band-basket-crawl (BBC) arrangement where each country chooses *different* weights in the basket, size of band and extent of crawl. Over time, if there is a convergence in trade and investment structures in the region, consideration could be given to the creation of a *common* BBC arrangement, which involves the management of the exchange rate against a common basket of currencies which includes the ACU, the US dollar and the Euro. The *eventual* aim would be to manage individual nominal exchange rates to maintain fluctuation of the common basket index within a band, so as to ensure relative stability of their effective exchange rates (Table 14.1).[4]

An important technical aspect of the ACU is the question of the economic indicators used to assign weights to determine the composition of the currency basket. Table 14.1 provides some initial estimates of the weights of the ACU, assuming membership spans ASEAN+6. The basket weights of the Asian currencies are based on an arithmetic average of two shares: (a) each country's regional share of GDP (measured both in terms of US dollars and PPP) and (b) each country's share of trade based on the average between 2002 and 2005. While the estimates are

*Table 14.1* Illustrative weights of the ACU

| | Share of regional trade | Share of regional GDP (USD) | Share of regional GDP (PPP) | Simple average of trade and GDP (USD) | Simple average of trade and GDP (PPP) |
|---|---|---|---|---|---|
| Australia | 5.05 | 6.10 | 3.61 | 5.78 | 4.33 |
| Brunei | 0.17 | 0.06 | N.A. | 0.12 | N.A. |
| Cambodia | 0.09 | 0.05 | 0.17 | 0.07 | 0.13 |
| China | 23.94 | 19.13 | 39.25 | 21.54 | 31.60 |
| Japan | 27.05 | 51.73 | 21.14 | 39.39 | 24.1 |
| India | 4.01 | 6.94 | 17.61 | 5.48 | 10.81 |
| Indonesia | 3.12 | 2.53 | 4.22 | 2.83 | 3.67 |
| South Korea | 11.58 | 7.10 | 5.38 | 9.34 | 8.48 |
| Malaysia | 5.98 | 1.23 | 1.36 | 3.61 | 3.67 |
| Myanmar | 0.18 | N.A. | N.A. | 0.18 | 0.18 |
| New Zealand | 1.04 | 0.88 | 0.55 | 0.96 | 0.80 |
| Philippines | 2.32 | 0.97 | 2.13 | 1.65 | 2.25 |
| Singapore | 9.20 | 1.15 | 0.64 | 5.18 | 4.92 |
| Thailand | 4.81 | 1.66 | 2.75 | 3.34 | 3.78 |
| Vietnam | 1.32 | 0.46 | 1.19 | 0.89 | 1.26 |

*Source*: A. Sen Gupta and A. Palit (2008). "Feasibility of an Asian Currency Unit", Working Paper No. 208, Indian Council for Research on International Economic Relations, New Delhi.

indicative, clearly much more work needs to be done on developing alternative methodologies to determine appropriate basket weights.

Clearly it would be premature to consider harmonisation of Asian exchange rate and monetary policies to a common currency basket at this stage (let alone a currency union based on the ACU) when neither the economic nor the political preconditions exist for doing so. Attempting rigid policy coordination before the necessary preconditions are met would be like putting the cart before the horse; it is doomed to fail. While the ACU cannot be viewed as an attractive nominal anchor for Asian currencies in the near term, it could have a role to play in Asian monetary and financial cooperation in the future. This in turn should help the region gain a greater degree of economic resilience and reduce its heavy dependence on the US dollar and the US economy.

# 15
# Asia in the G20: Monetary and Financial Considerations

*(with Sasidaran Gopalan)*

The global financial crisis (GFC) has once again made it apparent that sound macroeconomic and financial fundamentals are necessary but not sufficient conditions for a country to remain immune from capital account shocks. Openness to trade and financial flows offers significant benefits in terms of, for example, enhancement of product competition, productivity improvements, variety in goods and services, risk diversification, but it also leaves a country vulnerable to external shocks of various types. The challenge for policymakers is to put in place adequate and effective financial safeguards against such shocks. This is especially important for highly open economies in Asia that have limited domestic social safety nets.

The *Group of 20* (G20), which was created in response to the spate of financial crises in the late 1990s as well as in recognition of the shift in world power to the fast-growing emerging market economies (Table 15.1), seems to be a useful forum for the discussion of some of the ongoing monetary, financial and governance-related concerns of emerging economies in Asia and elsewhere.[1] Asia has a unique opportunity to ensure that the G20's agenda is focused more on emerging economies, rather than being driven largely by the interests of the industrialised group of countries (G7). Indeed, South Korea itself has pushed for the creation of an "East Asian caucus" of the G20 that would comprise six members from the region – Australia, China, India, Indonesia, Japan and South Korea. This, along with the possible regularisation of an ASEAN representative (as in the case of the EU) at the meetings would give a significant fillip to a unified Asian voice/position in the G20, and help move forward some of the issues of central importance to the region.

*Table 15.1* What the world (US, Eurozone and China) may look like in 2030

| | US | | Eurozone-16 | | China | |
|---|---|---|---|---|---|---|
| | 2009 | 2030(f) | 2009 | 2030(f) | 2009 | 2030(f) |
| Population (million) | 309 | 369 | 321 | 289 | 1,337 | 1,462 |
| GDP (USD trillion) | 14.3 | 35.3 | 12.5 | 23.6 | 4.9 | 39.4 |
| Trade[a] (USD trillion) | 2.7 | 6.6 | 3.1[b] | 4.7[b] | 2.2 | 17.7 |
| Govt. bond market (USD trillion) | 9.2 | 28.3 | 8.0 | 18.9 | 1.4 | 19.7 |

*Notes:* [a] Merchandise trade only. [b] Extra-EU 27.

*Source*: M. Jaeger (2010). "Yuan as a Reserve Currency: Likely Prospects and Possible Implications", Deutsche Bank Research, July 16.

The G20 has taken some noteworthy initiatives, including the coordination of global fiscal expansion to combat the GFC as well as the establishment of the Financial Stability Board (FSB) as a step towards enhancing financial stability.[2] In other cases, while the G20 has made wide-ranging proclamations since 1999, they have not always been translated into action.[3] The "credibility deficit" of the G20 is likely to be a serious issue in forthcoming summits and can be addressed only if concrete measures are taken to devise a roadmap and design supporting institutions (such as a secretariat) to carry out the decisions made during the earlier summits.

While the leaders of the G20 have focused on the GFC and short-term crisis management issues, the IMF's Deputy Managing Director John Lipsky has rightly noted that there are three "architectural issues" that should be given high priority at future summits. We quote him below:[4]

> The international financial system needs to be made more robust ... (T)here is a need to accelerate the process of strengthening both regulatory and supervisory elements.
>
> The resilience of the international system needs to be improved. A strengthened global financial safety net is an important potential building block.
>
> Governance reform at the IMF is another challenge. With an objective set in Pittsburgh, all eyes are turning to Seoul for delivery. But quota reform is only one aspect of the task. A broader reform package is needed to adequately reflect new economic realities.

While six of the G20 countries are from the Asia-Pacific region, the region has just over 20 percent of IMF voting shares and this obvious anomaly needs to be addressed with greater conviction in the forthcoming summit. Appropriate IMF reforms – initiated by the G20 under Chinese chairmanship in 2006 – are needed to ensure that Asia's voting shares and its overall representation in and governance of the IMF are more in line with Asia's contribution to the world economy.[5] In the run-up to the G20 leaders' meeting in Seoul, the finance ministers did agree to move forward on some reforms of IMF governance structures, primarily in terms of rebalancing IMF quotas in favour of developing countries.[6] While this is a good start, much more remains to be done with regard to such questions as the executive board leadership, US veto power and the appointment of a managing director.

Reforms of global economic governance must be supplemented by strengthening regional institutions such as the CMIM (see Chapter 13). Asia, having undergone significant financial sector restructuring following the Asian financial crisis a decade before the GFC, should play a much more proactive role in reforming the financial regulatory system, including the creation of a new global regime for bank capital, liquidity and accounting.

While emerging markets are well represented, thus far they appear to have allowed the advanced countries to drive the G20 process. This is largely due to the failure of the emerging economies within the G20 to table unified positions. Appropriate steps need to be taken to ensure that their interests and stakes are not marginalised in the process.[7] With the ongoing *shift* in the *global centre* of gravity to Asia (which the GFC has probably hastened), it is going to be crucial that the upcoming and future G20 summits recognise the importance of bringing on board the interests of the Asian countries.

In this context, the Korean proposal to create an "East Asian caucus" of the G20 would be an important development if it helps Asia to organise itself better and speak with a more unified voice in the G20 and drive the agenda. However, such a caucus should make sure that it is inclusive and includes the concerns of non-Asian emerging economies. Indeed, given that the G20 is essentially an informal inter-governmental coordination body with no executive power, it is imperative that it gains broad-based legitimacy from global governance at the highest political level. Therefore, it is of the utmost importance that the interests and needs of the non-G20 countries are sufficiently represented and included in the discussions. For this to happen, the members of the G20 should initiate and promote dialogue with the other non-G20 countries whenever possible to take on board their views. For instance, the decision of the ASEAN member countries to organise a contact group that would collect and coordinate the different perspectives and positions within ASEAN countries (that are not a part of the G20) regarding the forthcoming G20 meetings is a step in that direction.

To enhance the G20's legitimacy, Korea has invited five countries to attend the upcoming Seoul meeting – Ethiopia (chair of the New Partnership for African Development), Malawi (chair of the African Union), Singapore (chair of the Global Governance Group), Vietnam (chair of ASEAN) and Spain (seemingly by default, as it has been invited to previous meetings).[8]

Back in 2002, the G20 members created "five notional groups of countries" from which the G20 chair for each year would be selected. The current year's chairmanship was drawn from the *Group 5* set of countries consisting of the four East Asian economies – South Korea, Japan, Indonesia and China. India belongs to *Group 2*: the emerging economies along with Russia, South Africa and Turkey. India, Brazil and South Africa (IBSA) are also members of the IBSA Dialogue Forum whose aim is to promote international cooperation among the three countries and the three continents of Asia, Africa and Latin America. India can therefore play an important bridging role between the Asian countries (East Asian caucus) and the non-Asian emerging economies,[9] but it needs to be much more constructively proactive in the G20 process.

# Part IV

# Monetary and Financial Issues in India

# 16
# The Global Financial Crisis and the Bank Lending Channel[1]

*(with M. Shahidul Islam)*

Bank lending is an important but oft-neglected channel through which monetary policy affects the overall economy. A large number of firms, particularly small and medium-sized enterprises (SMEs), depend on commercial banks for funding. The basic idea behind the bank lending channel is as follows: an expansionary monetary policy raises the excess reserves of banks, leading to lower bank lending rates, hence increasing bank lending and economic activity. The bank lending channel works quite effectively during normal circumstances. However, during a situation of bank distress, infusions of liquidity into the banking system may not readily translate into a rise in bank lending as banks become highly risk averse – especially in the face of growing non-performing loans (NPLs) and eroding capital bases (the "capital crunch") – and choose instead to hoard funds. This in turn implies no change in bank lending rates or the quantity of bank lending.

It is, of course, possible that due to moral suasion from the central bank, or for some other reason, banks may feel obliged to lower lending rates. However, if this is the case, they could still choose to restrict lending. While some might interpret this situation as one of disequilibrium, i.e. a mandated ceiling interest rate, causing an excess of demand over supply, from a bank's perspective, they may view effective demand as having declined as there are fewer credit-worthy customers who would qualify for bank loans.

This is a situation where monetary policy transmission breaks down in the sense that liquidity infused into the banking system by the central bank does not find its way to the rest of the economy; credit is clogged up in the banks. This is the classic credit crunch, where the problem is not so much the *cost of funds* but the *availability of funds*, and there is endless debate about whether the lack of credit creation is because banks are not lending or because – as perceived by the banks – there are not enough "credit-worthy" customers. The relevant point here, however, is that increases in reserve money without any corresponding expansion of broad money will show up as a decline in broad money multiplier – the ratio of broad money to base money.

*The bank lending story in the US:* In the case of the US, as part of the programme of monetary easing in response to the crisis, the Fed funds rate was cut to its lower bound (setting a target between 0 and 0.25 percent) and the bank prime loan rate in the US subsequently declined in line with that cut (Figure 16.1). However, there was a sharp rise in the LIBOR-OIS spread (a measure of the degree of risk aversion of banks) in September–October 2008 (Figure 16.2). Given this risk aversion, banks were not extending credit to the public, choosing instead to hoard reserves or place them in government securities, consequently leading to a drop in the money multiplier (Figure 16.3). More precisely, thanks to a massive credit-easing programme, the monetary base (M0) in the US more than doubled from USD 843 billion in August 2008 to USD 1.75 trillion in May 2009. However, broad money growth did

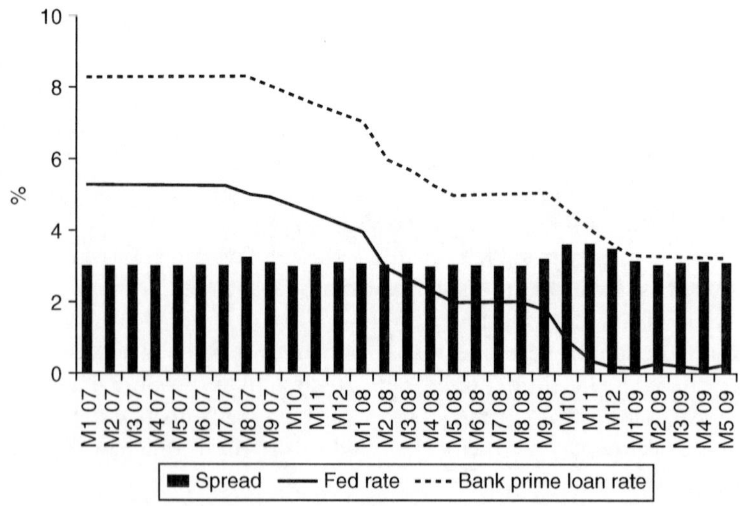


*Figure 16.1* The spread between Fed fund rate and the US bank prime loan rate, M1:2007–M5:2009

*Source*: Based on the Federal Reserve Bank of St. Louis, USA.

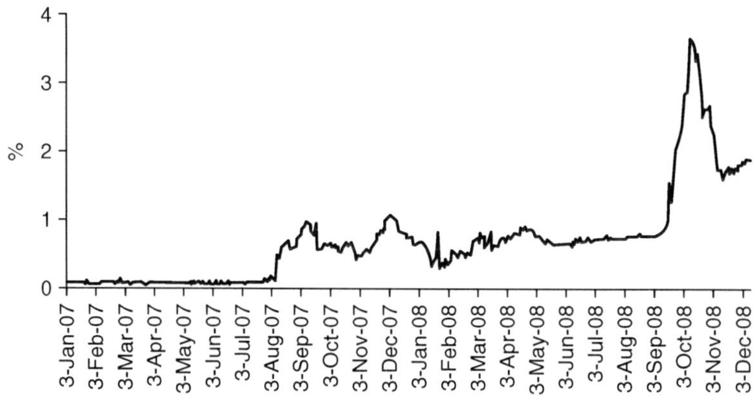


*Figure 16.2* LIBOR–OIS spread on daily basis, M1:2007–M12:2008

*Source*: Based on the Federal Reserve Bank of St. Louis, USA, and the British Banker's Association.

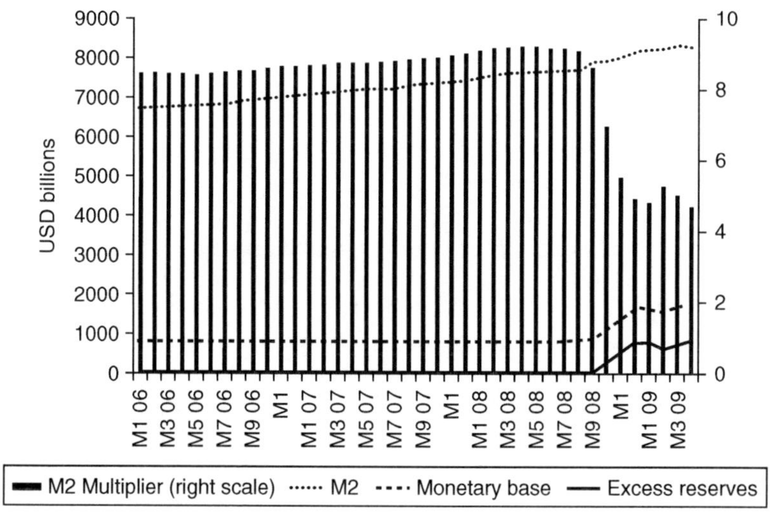


*Figure 16.3* Trends in monetary base, broad money, excess reserves and M2 multiplier in the US, M1:2006–M4:2009

*Source*: Based on the Federal Reserve Bank of St. Louis, USA.

not increase at the same pace. As a result, the money multiplier collapsed from 9.1 in August 2008 to 4.7 in April 2009 and the gigantic increase in the Fed balance sheet did not translate into credit growth, as banks chose to hold the excess reserves rather than make loans to the private sector. (It also suggests that inflation concerns were overplayed initially, as broad monetary growth did not blow up – unlike narrow money.)

*The bank lending story in India:* The global financial crisis (GFC) hit India initially through the financial channels, particularly following the collapse of Lehman Brothers in September 2008 and consequent global deleveraging. Many Indian corporates that had depended on global wholesale markets for "cheap" foreign currency funding suddenly found themselves facing a major liquidity crisis: credit dried up as concerns about counterparty risks sky-rocketed. As these entities turned to domestic banks and nonbanks (such as mutual fund withdrawals) to refinance so as to remain liquid, there were huge pressures on domestic sources of liquidity.

In the case of the banking sector, these pressures were most clearly reflected in the sharp rise in volatilities in the Indian call money market. The destruction of wealth in India and globally due to asset price declines, as well as the increased cost of credit, inevitably caused the country's export growth to plunge and industrial production to decelerate in August–November 2008 (Figure 16.4). As the gravity of the financial crisis became apparent, from mid-September–October 2008, the RBI took several policy measures to ease both the Rupee and the foreign exchange liquidity conditions in the financial system. The RBI reduced the key policy rates (the repo and the reverse repo), while the cash reserve requirement (CRR) was cut sharply, along with other measures to ease domestic liquidity sharply (Figure 16.5). Foreign exchange liquidity was also eased by loosening restrictions on external commercial borrowings (ECBs) and short-term trade credits, while interest rate ceilings on nonresident deposits were raised in order to attract more foreign funds into the country.

How did these monetary measures affect the growth of reserve money, broad money and non-food credit? After June 2008, the growth of reserve money declined sharply (year-on-year) until March 2009 (Figure 16.6). The two main reasons for this were the decline in net foreign assets (NFA) due to a loss of foreign exchange reserves and, more importantly, the decline in the CRR, which implied lower net domestic assets (NDAs) due to a fall in bank reserves with the RBI. Infusions of

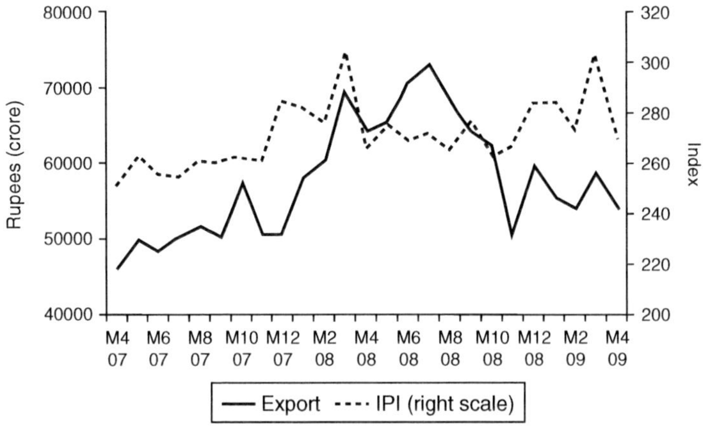


*Figure 16.4* Trends in export and industrial production index, M4:2007–M4:2009

*Source*: Based on the Reserve Bank of India and the Ministry of Statistics and Programme Implementation, Government of India.

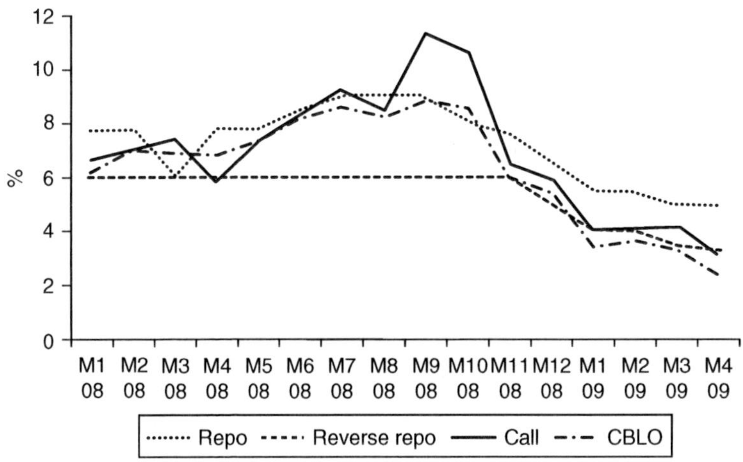


*Figure 16.5* Trends in repo, reverse repo and call money and CBLO rate, M1:2008–M4:2009

*Source*: Based on the Reserve Bank of India and the Clearing Corporation of India Ltd.

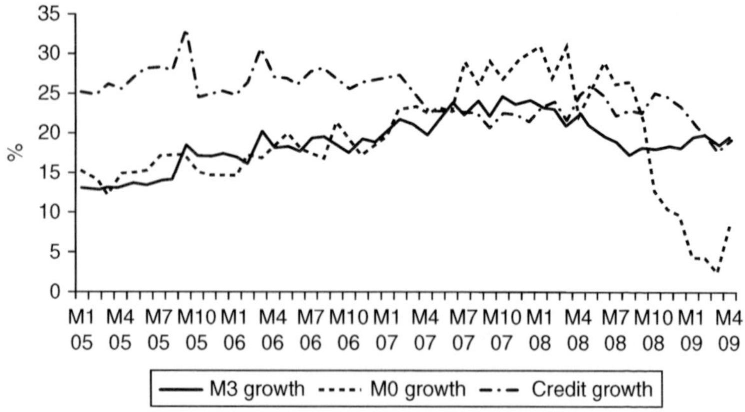


*Figure 16.6* Year-on-year growth in base money, broad money and commercial credit, M1:2005–M4:2009

*Source*: Based on Reserve Bank of India.

liquidity by the RBI helped to partially offset some of these declines. More important for the economy was the fact that credit and broad money continued to grow at a stable and robust rate. The decline in reserve money and consequent increase in broad money inevitably implied a sudden rise in the money multiplier (Figure 16.7), in sharp contrast to the US. The fact that credit was rising robustly implies that there was no significant credit crunch in India during the period under consideration.

*The bank lending conundrum in India:* Overall, the monetary measures taken clearly eased the liquidity crunch in India. The added liquidity has partly offset the drying-up of nonbank sources of funds. But despite the seeming success of RBI's policy interventions for offsetting any potential credit crunch, surprisingly, bank lending rate has not declined in line with the RBI's credit-easing policies. The repo rate has declined sharply but the prime lending rate has not fallen at the same pace, with the result that the spread between the two rates remains high.[2]

Conceptually, one can reconcile these seemingly contradictory facts – robust lending but downward rigidity in lending rates – if one believes that the increase in supply of loans was also matched by an increase in demand, such that overall lending grows but there is little or no change in lending rates. As noted, in the case of India, there was a significant

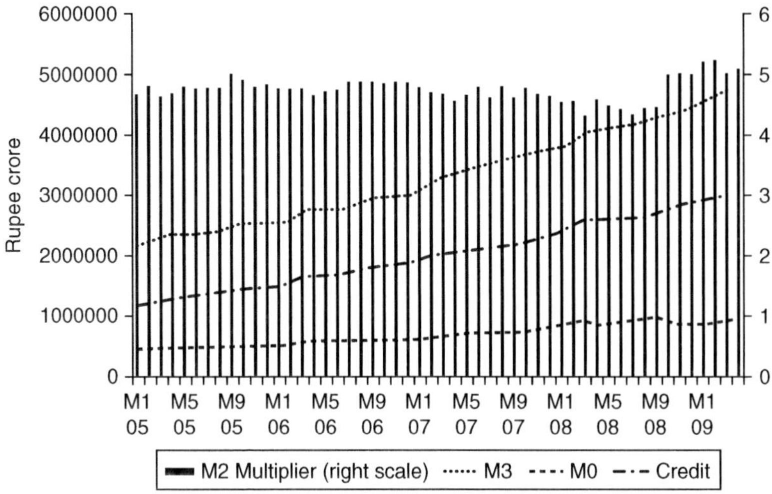


*Figure 16.7* Trends in base money, broad money, credit and broad money multiplier in India, M1:2005–M4:2009

*Source*: Based on Reserve Bank of India.

rise in demand for funds domestically as many corporates shifted from overseas borrowing (which had dried up) to domestic sources, including banks. In addition, there are some structural issues concerning further downward adjustments in *benchmark prime lending rates* (BPLR), as they are linked to the rate of inflation and deposit rates. Also, the bulk of banks' time deposits continue to be at fixed interest rates. Banks may, therefore, need some time to re-price their loans.

Apart from structural problems that hinder the reduction of the BPLR, the other issue has to do with effectiveness of moral suasion. The RBI has been able to influence the public sector banks, which accounted for over 70 percent loan growth in 2008–09, to reduce BPLR and increase the credit flows, but private and foreign commercial banks have been rather reluctant or slow to respond to such calls. Both the private sector and foreign commercial banks showed clear conservatism, in terms of increasing credit flows to the private sector in March 2008–09 (Table 16.1). Private and foreign banks seem to have chosen to park some of the excess liquidity at the RBI's reverse repo window and invest in government securities rather than lend it out.

*Table 16.1* Credit flows from scheduled commercial banks (in percentage, year-on-year changes)

| | January 4, 2008 | January 4, 2009 | March 28, 2008 | March 28, 2009 |
|---|---|---|---|---|
| **Public sector banks** | 19.8 | 28.6 | 22.5 | 20.4 |
| **Private banks** | 24.2 | 11.8 | 19.9 | 10.9 |
| **Foreign banks** | 30.7 | 16.9 | 28.5 | 4.0 |

*Source*: Macroeconomic and Monetary Development, various Issues, RBI.

Bank lending will always remain an important source of finance for SMEs which may not be able to access alternative sources. However, the global liquidity crisis has emphasised that during the period of acute global risk aversion and distress, domestic banks in India were crucial as sources of finance, even to large corporates that might otherwise raise funds in the international capital markets. The bank lending channel in India operated fairly well in the midst of the global credit crunch, and India does not appear to have faced as severe a domestic credit crunch as that of the US and elsewhere. This in turn may have been because the Indian banking sector is largely controlled by the public sector banks (in terms of total assets, deposits and advances).[3] These public banks have been more responsive to the RBI's moral suasion and other credit-easing measures than the private sector banks – particularly foreign banks – which have shown severe conservatism in terms of bank lending during the crisis period. This may have lessons for further liberalisation of India's banking sector in the future, though these possible macro stability gains must be traded off against possible microeconomic benefits from greater private sector competition.

# 17 Macroeconomic Management during a Period of Plenty in India

There are two indisputable facts about India and the global financial crisis (GFC) of 2008–09. One, India was far more heavily impacted by the global financial turmoil than most informed observers expected. This clearly attests to the significant increase in the extent of India's financial and trade openness with the rest of the world. Two, the Indian economy bounced back from the crisis more rapidly than most other countries. Apart from stimulative demand-management policies, the recovery highlighted the importance of the domestic market to India's overall growth, as well as the soundness and stability of its banking and overall financial system, which is a testament to the country's conservative approach to regulatory policies.

The sharpness of Indian's economic rebound, its overall resilience, along with the lowering of global risk aversion, once again led to a surge in foreign capital inflows into the country. To be sure, India has continued to run a current account deficit that has been gradually rising and now stands at around 3 percent of GDP, something last seen in 1990–91. In contrast, in 2009–10, India ran a much larger capital account surplus of about 3.8 percent of GDP (Table 17.1), fuelled both by foreign direct investments (FDIs) and foreign portfolio investments (FPIs), the latter consisting mainly of foreign institutional investments (FIIs) (Figure 17.1).

According to RBI data, net FPIs into India between April and December 2009 rose sharply to around USD 23.5 billion, compared with a net outflow of just over USD 14 billion in 2008. This, in turn, helped push the local stock market to a two-year high and also put upward pressure on the Indian Rupee (notwithstanding the retreat in May 2010 largely because of the strength of the US dollar) (Figure 17.2). India thus found itself in the pre-GFC era of 2007–08 when it was faced with the "problem of plenty".

*Table 17.1* Trends in India's external sector

| | 2006–07 | 2007–08 | 2008–09 | 2009–10 |
|---|---|---|---|---|
| Current account deficit (percentage of GDP) | 1.0 | 1.3 | 2.4 | 2.5 |
| Net capital flows (percentage of GDP) | 4.8 | 8.7 | 0.6 | 3.8 |
| Capital flows in excess of current account deficit (billions of dollars) | 36 | 92 | –20 | 14 |
| Rupee appreciation (+) depreciation (–) vis-à-vis US dollar during the year | 2.3 | 9.0 | –21.5 | 12.9 |

*Note*: Numbers for 2009–10 are rough estimates.
*Source*: Reproduced from D. Subbarao (2010). "India and the Global Financial Crisis – Transcending from Recovery to Growth", remarks at the Peterson Institute of International Economics, Washington DC, April 26, 2010, available at www.iie.com/publications/papers/paper.cfm?ResearchID=1556

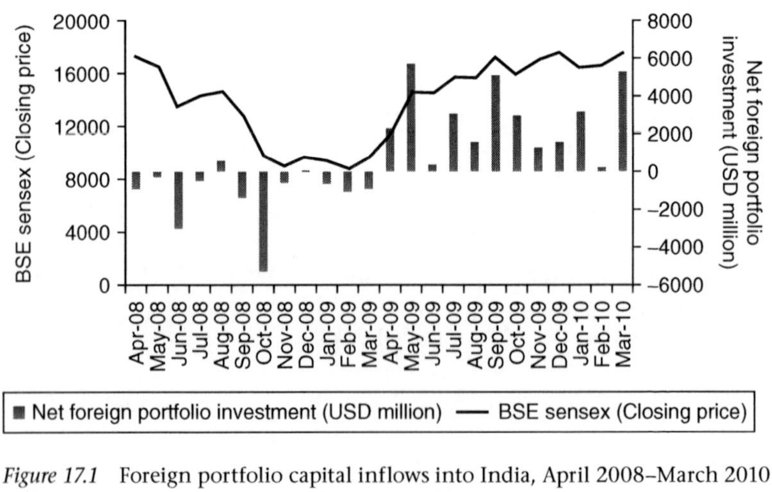


*Figure 17.1* Foreign portfolio capital inflows into India, April 2008–March 2010
*Source*: Reserve Bank of India Monthly Bulletin; BSE Indices, Bombay Stock Exchange.

Large-scale capital inflows can be managed in a number of ways. One option is to limit the size of the capital account surplus through a combination of policies that promote capital outflows, while also moderating the size of capital inflows through capital controls (see Chapter 7). While India attempted to do the former in 2007–08, it has rightly been

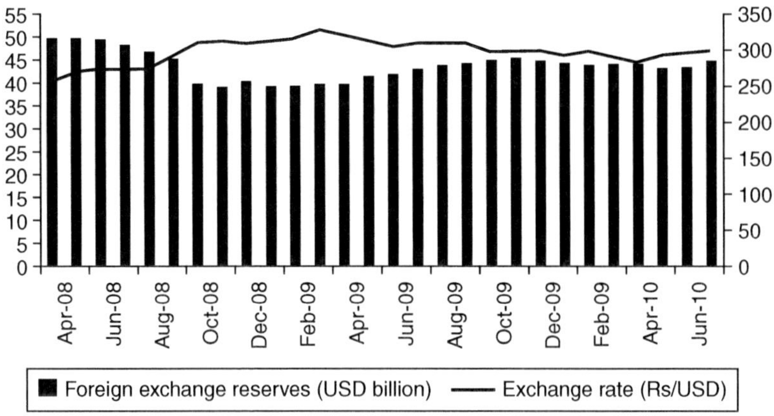


*Figure 17.2* India's foreign exchange reserves and US dollar exchange rate, April 2008–April 2010

*Source*: Reserve Bank of India Monthly Bulletin; Pacific Exchange Rate database.

somewhat more cautious about being too aggressive in further liberalising capital outflows post-GFC, lest it be faced with another sudden shock and capital flight.

This seems to leave capital controls as the obvious option, one that has been talked about for some time in India, especially in the form of administrative curbs on external commercial borrowings (ECBs). There has also been some discussion of Brazilian-, Chilean- or Colombian-type market-based controls. However, as of end 2010, no obvious policy decision had been taken on capital controls. Part of the concern here is to what extent such piecemeal controls can, in fact, be effective: for instance, there is some evidence to suggest that, while controls tend to lengthen the maturity of capital inflows (thus presumably reducing the chance of booms and busts), they also, to some degree, disproportionately raise the cost of credit to small-and-medium-sized enterprises (SMEs) (see Chapter 7).

Owing to the absence of any credible attempts to control net capital inflows, there was some sharp upward pressure on the Indian Rupee; it reached Rs 52 per US dollar level (in March 2009) during the height of the GFC, and hovered at around Rs 47 to the US dollar as of mid-May 2010. Between April 2009 and April 2010, the Rupee appreciated by about 15 percent against a trade-weighted basket of currencies, moderated somewhat by the strength of the US dollar in May 2010. In contrast, the Chinese Renminbi depreciated by about 5 percent against its trading partners over the same period (Figure 17.3). This relatively sharp appreciation of the Rupee has led to concerns about its possible negative impacts on India's external competitiveness as an export and investment hub.

Consistent with its policy of managed floating, the RBI has, in the past, intervened in the foreign exchange market to control – rather than prevent – Rupee appreciation. This was certainly the case between April 2009 and November 2009, when India's reserves rose from USD 250 billion to around USD 290 billion. However, since then the reserves have remained fairly stable, implying that the RBI has eschewed any significant foreign exchange intervention and has, since December 2009, permitted the Rupee to finds its own level in the market.

Part of the appreciation of the Rupee is consistent with the fact that the authorities had also let the currency move downwards during the global crisis, compared to the Renminbi. However, given the extent of the rise of the Indian Rupee, members of the exporting sectors (such as diamonds, textiles and the IT industry) voiced concerns about the loss of competitiveness. The Confederation of Indian Industry (CII) called upon the RBI to intervene in the currency markets, arguing that failure to do so would derail the export recovery which only began in November 2009 (the economy having contracted over the preceding two years).

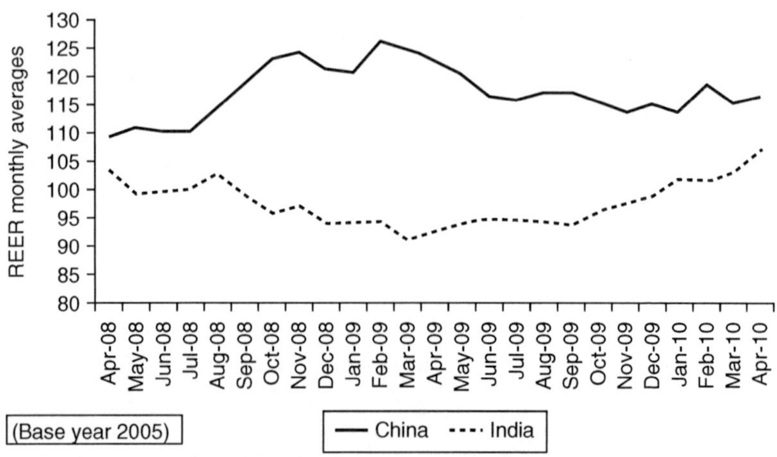


*Figure 17.3* REER of India and China, April 2008–April 2010
*Source*: BIS Effective Exchange Rate Database.

There were also concerns that the rising Rupee might limit the extent of inward remittance flows from the Middle-East and elsewhere, all of which would further widen India's current account deficit.

Against this, the Rupee appreciation has probably been tolerated by the RBI as a means of countering the inflationary effects of a rebound in global commodity prices and other tradable prices. Indeed, poor monsoon and rising agricultural prices have already worked in tandem to result in an upward inflationary bias in India and elsewhere (see Chapter 18). This near-double-digit increase, which in turn is raising inflationary expectations, is a cause for concern and is certainly outside the RBI's comfort zone.

Faced with such constraints, during the IMF and World Bank Spring meeting in Washington, DC in April 2010 the RBI Governor Duvvuri Subbarao reopened the debate about the virtues of including capital controls in the overall macroeconomic policy toolkit.[1] Whether this becomes actual policy or merely a means of curbing the enthusiasm of short-term foreign investment flows into India through words rather than deeds remains to be seen. The RBI may also re-enter the currency market to manage the currency's appreciation, though the side-effects of such a policy in terms of liquidity creation will also need to be carefully studied and effectively managed. Over the medium-term, though, the ideal solution would probably be to reign in the large fiscal expenditures as a means of reducing domestic demand and the pressures on domestic nontradable prices. Unfortunately, rampant fiscal expenditures (at the state level) continue to be India's Achilles heel.

# 18
# Post-Global Financial Crisis: Heating Up of the Inflation Debate in India

*(with Venkataramana Yanamandra)*

While the US and the other industrial countries continue to face the very real risk of a recession-deflation spiral due to their large output gaps (i.e. excess of potential output over actual output), some emerging economies in Asia are facing the problem of inflation due to overheating of the economy. The inflationary problem is particularly acute in India, which has experienced double digit inflation since the beginning of 2010 as the economy has been on a tear, growing by 7.4 percent in 2009–10 (Figure 18.1). Inflation as measured by the Wholesale Price Index (WPI), as measured by the new and old series, has been in double digits since February 2010.[1] Specifically, it peaked at 12.9 percent in August 2008 due to rising oil and commodity prices internationally and then declined sharply between March 2008 and June 2009, even turning negative for a period (due to a high base effect phenomenon in certain commodity groups such as iron and steel and fuels). The inflation rate turned positive in September 2009 and has been around 11 percent since February 2010. As of June 2010, y-o-y growth in the WPI was 10.6 percent as per the old series but there was a moderation in the price index since July according to both series.[2]

There are two main reasons for inflationary pressures in general: demand-pull factors and cost-push factors. The initial uptick in inflation in India was clearly due to supply-side factors caused by lower production of food grains: the drought in India from June to September of 2009 was one of the worst in the country since 1972. Higher food price inflation pushed up wages, as food items make up more than 50 percent

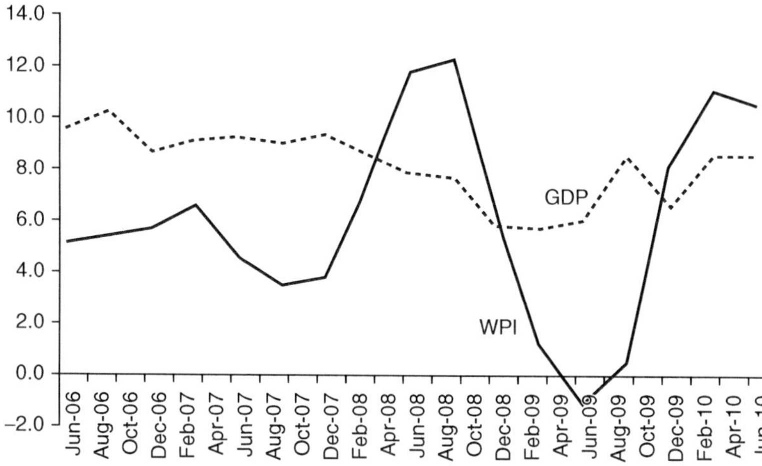


*Figure 18.1* GDP and WPI rates (year-on-year percentage change)

*Note*: While the CPI is a better gauge of household inflation, The WPI is preferred over the CPI in India due to its higher frequency of availability, i.e. weekly; the CPI is available less frequently, with lags.

*Source*: RBI *Macroeconomic and Monetary Developments*, various issues; Office of the Economic Adviser, Ministry of Commerce and Industry, GOI.

of the consumption basket. In addition, structural bottlenecks in certain perishable horticultural and animal husbandry commodities such as pulses, milk and vegetables also contributed to higher food prices in the country by worsening the supply-side distortions.

Looking at the various subcomponents, food article prices, both primary and manufactured, rose by 10.4 percent, fuels by 14.6 percent and manufactured non-food products by 7.3 percent, while non-food items inflation (WPI excluding food) was at 10.6 percent during June 2010. Within the food category, inflation in primary food items was at 14.6 percent, while that for food products was at 4.3 percent during June 2010 (Figures 18.2 and 18.3). As of August 2010, food articles were still among the main contributors to the WPI, rising by over 14 percent, with articles other than food contributing to around two-thirds of the inflation. Despite the fact that food prices contributed the most to inflation and that they experienced some moderation, non-food prices have also witnessed an uptick, signalling capacity constraints.[3]

Given the supply-side nature of the initial inflation spike, the RBI's direct role was limited. While the bank offered significant monetary

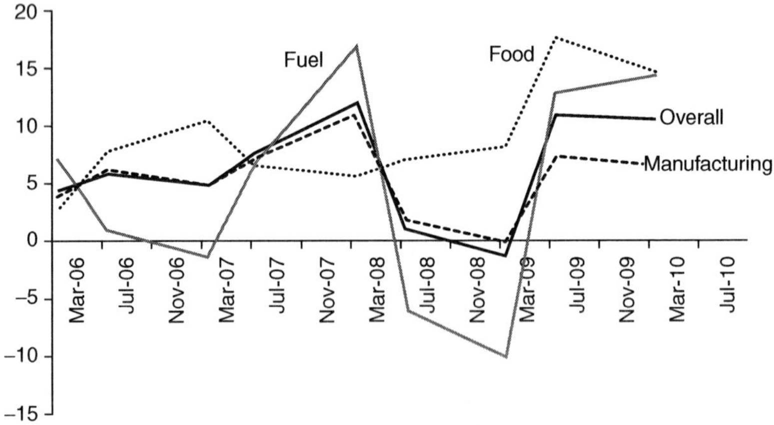


*Figure 18.2* WPI inflation (year-on-year percentage change)

*Source*: Office of the Economic Adviser, Ministry of Commerce and Industry, GOI.

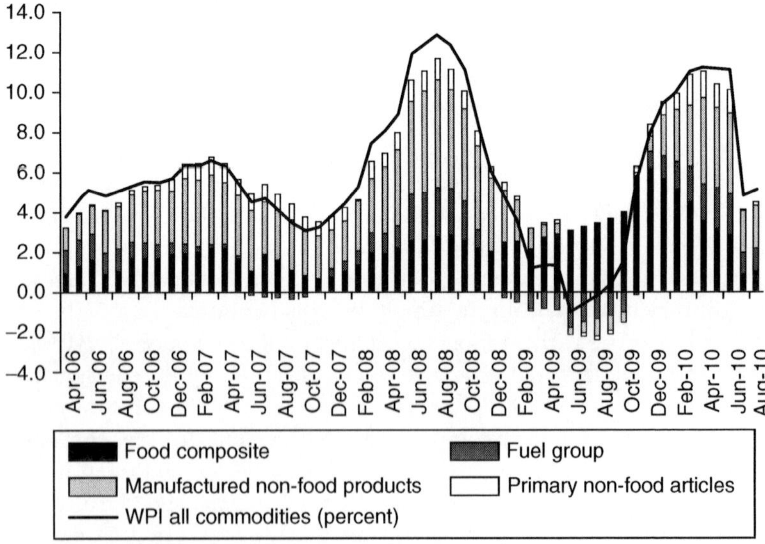


*Figure 18.3* Contribution of various components in WPI (year-on-year percentage change)

*Source*: Office of the Economic Adviser, Ministry of Commerce and Industry, GOI.

stimulus in the immediate aftermath of the global financial crisis (GFC) in October 2008 and beyond, it refrained from taking any significant action, despite inflationary concerns. This was largely because capital inflows into the country had not recovered to their pre-crisis levels, and there was a high level of uncertainty over the global financial and economic outlook. The RBI did, however, begin to withdraw some the crisis-induced monetary stimulus from October 2009 by raising the statutory liquidity ratio.

As noted, while the high levels of inflation initially originated from the supply-side in the second half of 2009–10, there has been a shift to demand-side factors since February 2010. This shift strengthened with a decline in the food prices in June 2010 due partly to the base effect, and in part due to the better monsoons. Indeed, the RBI in its Quarterly Report of July 27, 2010 identified capacity constraints in several sectors that were leading to a shortage of supply of commodities. This meant that there was a seller's market in those sectors, leading to rising inflation, despite a better monsoon than the previous year. In addition, the deregulation and increase in administered prices of petroleum products, along with the removal of fuel subsidies in June 2010, may have imparted some inflationary bias in the short term (though those factors are important from the perspective of long-term fiscal consolidation as well as energy conservation). This has raised fears of rising prices of petroleum products and essential commodities even further, and has led to large-scale protests in the country. According to RBI estimates, the deregulation will have an immediate direct effect of a 0.9 percentage point increase in WPI inflation in addition to a lagging indirect impact. Thus, despite the reduction in food price inflation and consumer price inflation, the RBI revised its WPI inflation forecast for March 2011 to 6 percent from 5.5 percent in April 2010.

Even though the country has experienced some moderation in the WPI, which dropped from 11 percent in April 2010 to 8.5 in August 2010, CPI growth remained stubbornly high during this period. In fact, the year-on-year CPI in May 2010 was, at 13.9 percent, one of the highest in Asia. The divergence between the WPI and CPI, which was at its peak during August 2009, has reduced due to the rise in the WPI index from the third quarter of 2009–10, largely because of the rise in food prices (Figure 18.4). The rise in the CPI was higher than that of the WPI because of the higher weight of food prices in this index – at an average of 46 percent for the CPI index compared to 27 percent for the WPI.

These high rates of inflation, which have been demand-induced since February 2010, have led to changes in the key policy interest rates. The RBI had taken some tentative steps towards normalising monetary policy (i.e. discontinuing its stimulus) in March 2010, when it raised the repo and reverse repo rates. It continued with these increases in April and May, each time raising the rates by 25 basis points.[4] Given the clear indication of cyclical recovery and demand-side pressures by mid-2010,

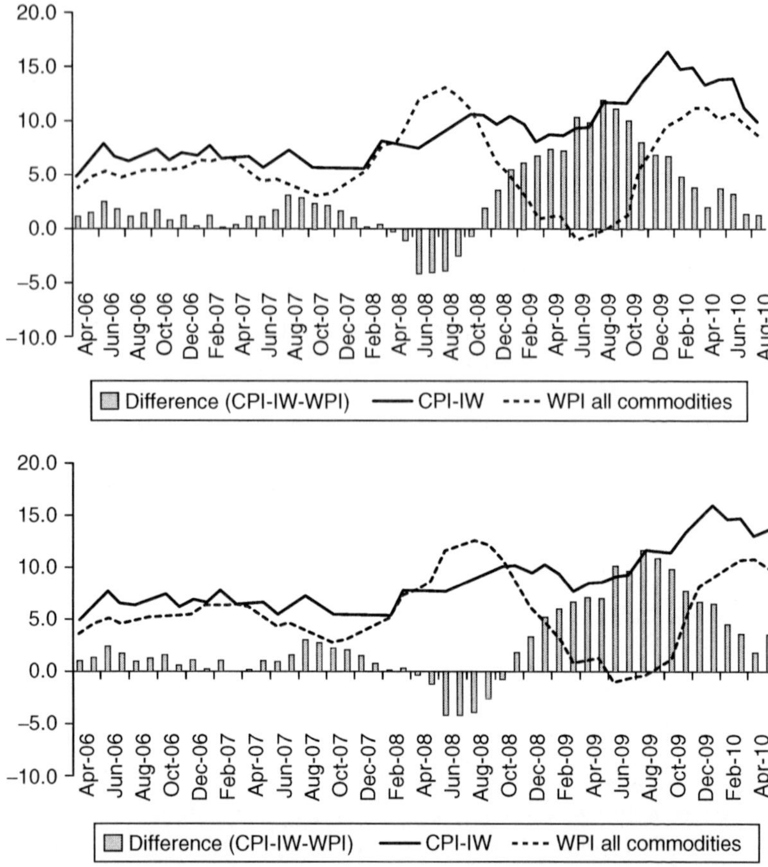


*Figure 18.4* CPI-IW and WPI inflation (year-on-year percentage change)
*Source*: RBI *Macroeconomic and Monetary Developments (Price Situation)*, various issues.

on July 27, 2010 the bank took more aggressive steps to keep the liquidity in the system tight by raising the reverse repo rate by 50 basis points to 4.50 percent and the repo rate by 25 basis points to 5.75 percent (Figure 18.5). The RBI further raised the repo rate by 25 basis points to 6.00 percent and the reverse repo by 50 basis points to 5.00 percent on September 16, 2010, despite the fact that the Indian economy was growing at the brisk pace of 8.8 percent.[5] Raising the reverse repo rate more than the repo is also an attempt to reduce the volatility in the overnight money market rate. The RBI's monetary policy statement also took on a much more hawkish tone, mainly to try and bring down inflationary

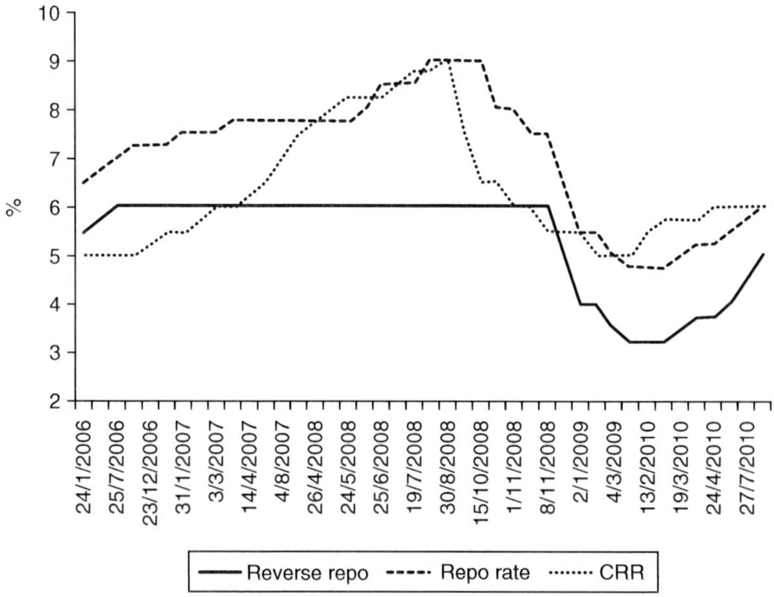


*Figure 18.5* Key policy rates (percentage)

*Source*: RBI *Macroeconomic and Monetary Developments*, various issues.

expectations. On the other hand, the RBI left the cash reserve ratio (CRR) unchanged at 6 percent.

The timing of the RBI move had come under criticism, given the decline in factory output as measured by the index of industrial production (IIP) in June 2010 (Figure 18.6). IIP growth started decelerating in May 2010 from a high of 17.6 percent y-o-y growth in April, and declined to a single digit growth rate in June 2010 (5.8 percent) for the first time since October 2009, before bouncing back to 13.8 percent in July 2010. Given that IIP growth had started declining even before the monetary tightening measures, rising interest rates are likely to hasten its slowdown. The high volatility of the index over June and July raises questions on the effectiveness of the index, but a case can be made that IIP growth had been unusually high in the recent past (due to inventory restocking), and moderation to 7–9 percent is a sustainable level for India. The combination of withdrawal of fiscal stimulus and rising interest rates will probably keep IIP growth in check in the future.

Given persistently high inflation in India, the effectiveness of monetary policy in controlling rising prices has been a question of debate. No

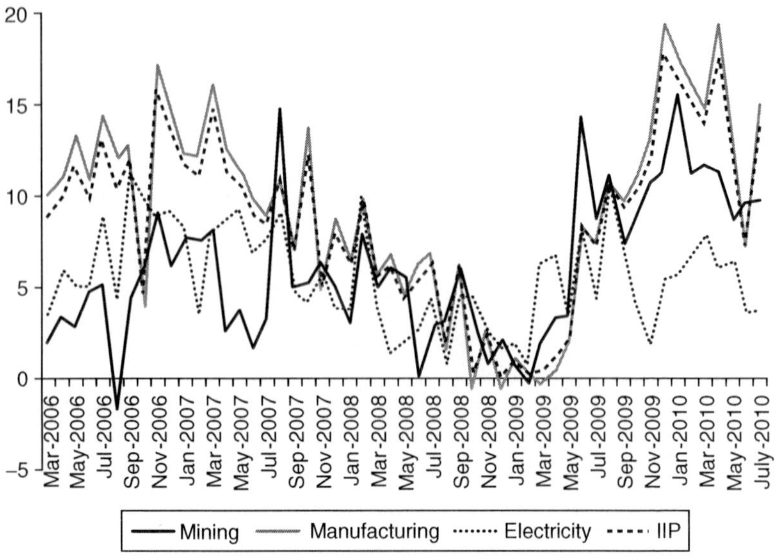


*Figure 18.6* IIP in India (year-on-year percentage change)
*Source*: Ministry of Statistics and Implementation, Government of India.

central bank in the world can use conventional monetary policy instruments to effectively tackle cost-push inflation. Insofar as demand-side factors have contributed to sustained high inflation in India, the RBI has increased the repo and the reverse repo rates to keep liquidity in the system tight, and has made clear its intention to maintain a tightening bias in monetary policy in the foreseeable future. The near-term challenge is to ensure that the RBI is able to alleviate inflationary pressures, while ensuring growth and industrial production are not choked off.

However, there are some medium- and longer-term concerns about the effectiveness of the RBI's instruments even to tackle demand-pull inflation. Indeed, the RBI governor Dr. D. Subbarao himself noted the following:

> A necessary condition for inflation targeting to work is effective monetary transmission. Our monetary transmission mechanism is improving but is yet to reach robust standards. It remains impeded because of administered interest rates, the asymmetric contractual relationship between banks and their depositors, illiquid bond markets and large government borrowings. These impediments to monetary transmission diminish our effectiveness as inflation targeters.[6]

More to the point, market interest rates have only limited sensitivity to the changes in policy rates used by the RBI. Even if there were an impact, a host of other distortions and price controls limit the transmission of interest rate changes into domestic prices. In addition, the continued large fiscal deficit – while not unsustainable in and of itself as long as growth remains buoyant – will impart an inflationary bias to the economy, which monetary policy will constantly need to counteract. Conscious efforts must be made to improve the effectiveness of the conventional interest rates transmission mechanism, both to domestic market interest rates and to final prices. The latter in turn requires that a host of structural distortions and rigidities in the Indian economy that go well beyond the purview of the RBI (agricultural prices, etc.) be addressed.

The concern is that another poor monsoon could once again push up inflation rates and render the RBI relatively ineffective, as its policy tools are only effective in curtailing demand. The government can help moderate price increases for at least some agricultural commodities by addressing the inefficiencies in the post-harvest value supply chain of these products. This would also help control exploitation of production-induced food scarcity by intermediaries. It can also control food price inflation to a certain extent by encouraging "organised retail" to sell food products, as these retailers are able to achieve economies of scale in procurement, handling and logistics and thus supply at lower prices than traditional retailers.

Given the high growth trajectory of the Indian economy, failure to tackle these rigidities could keep inflation stubbornly high, which in turn could have negative socio-political repercussions over time.

# 19
# India's International Reserves: How Diversified?[1]

*(with Sasidaran Gopalan)*

India has been stockpiling international reserves at an impressive pace during the last two decades or so. Reserves have sky-rocketed from around USD 5–6 million in 1991 to nearly USD 300 billion in mid-2008, among the highest in the world after China and Japan. India's reserves took a dip in mid-2008, following the reversal of capital flows induced by the global financial crisis as the RBI attempted a partial defense of the Indian Rupee to moderate the pace of its depreciation. However, as the crisis abated and the country saw the Congress-led government return to power in May 2009, foreign capital has begun surging back to India once again, helping the country to rapidly rebuild its foreign exchange reserves (Figure 19.1).

Given the massive stock of India's reserve holdings, many research studies have focused on issues concerning reserve adequacy, their determinants and the associated costs of holding of such reserves. Insufficient attention has, however, been paid to the composition of such reserves. This issue has taken on greater importance since November 2009 with the RBI's much-publicised purchase of 200 metric tons worth of gold from the IMF, estimated roughly at USD 6.7 billion at that time. Many observers have viewed this purchase as a conscious diversification strategy adopted by India to move away from investing in US dollar-denominated assets.

India's reserve assets primarily comprise foreign securities, foreign currency deposits and currencies, and gold deposits. Available data from the RBI offer some useful insights into reserve management in India (Figure 19.2). On average, over time, more than 50 percent of India's total reserve holdings have been in the form of foreign currencies and deposits as cash, followed by investments in foreign securities and then gold deposits, in that order. The large share in cash and deposits emphasises the RBI's high level of risk aversion in the management

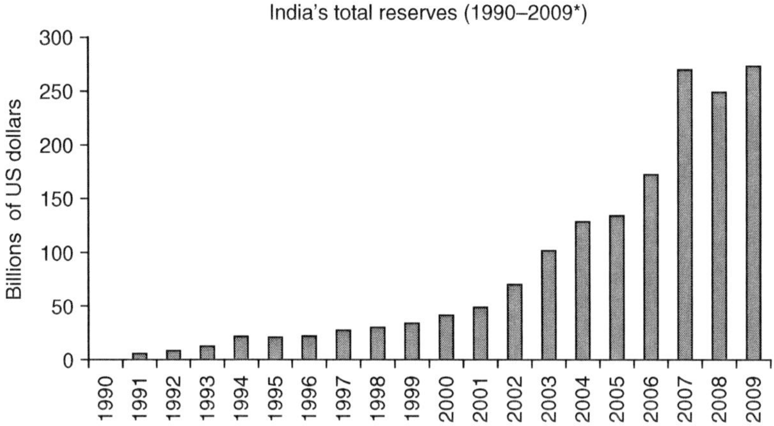


*Figure 19.1* Trends in India's total international reserves, 1990–2009*

*Note*: *September 2009.

*Source*: Compiled from CEIC data.

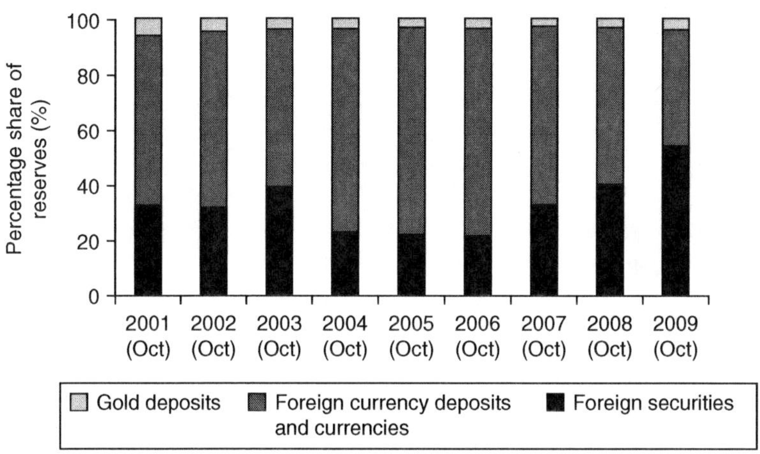


*Figure 19.2* India's international reserves: where are they invested?

*Source*: Compiled from the Reserve Bank of India.

of its reserves – liquidity management seems to be of paramount importance, regardless of the opportunity and fiscal costs involved in such a strategy.

It is interesting to note that the RBI allowed its share of reserves held in foreign securities to increase vis-à-vis currency deposits only after October 2007 – at the height of the global liquidity-induced bull run and just before the onset of the global financial crisis. The share of aggregate reserves parked in foreign securities stood at over 50 percent in October 2009, compared to around 33 percent in October 2007.

Can we say anything about the currency composition of these assets? Unfortunately things become rather fuzzy here, due to a severe lack of data. As with most other central banks, the currency composition of India's international reserves is a closely guarded secret. The only available source of information is the IMF database on the Currency Composition of Official Foreign Exchange Reserves (COFER) which provides this information as aggregates for groups of countries. While the available data from COFER seem to suggest that the share of US dollar assets held by emerging and developing economies stood at close to 60 percent as of end 2008, there is some anecdotal evidence to suggest that India has somewhat less of its reserves invested in US dollar assets than China and its East Asian neighbours, and this makes sense given India's more diversified trade structure. But there is nothing concrete that anyone can point to in order to substantiate this claim.

The RBI does, however, provide some information publicly, which will get us started. Using their data on valuation changes from reserve holdings from year-to-year, one can attempt some simulation exercises to arrive at reasonable guesstimates of India's non-gold reserve composition. Having undertaken such an exercise in a longer research paper,[2] our computations suggest that India invests about 40 percent of its aggregate reserve holdings in US dollars, 25 percent in Euros and the remainder divided among other currencies such as the Yen, Pound Sterling, Swiss Franc and Australian and Canadian dollars. Thus, although India seems to have parked a large share of its reserve holdings in US dollars, this share appears to be lower compared to the average among emerging and developing economies.

It is important to note that the share of India's aggregate reserves invested in gold has also been small, and has actually declined from about 6.5 percent in 2001 to about 3 percent in 2007. In October 2009, before India purchased gold from the IMF, the share of gold deposits in India's total reserves stood at around 4 percent, compared with 2 percent for other emerging economies and close to 1 percent for countries such as China. Following the gold purchase, India's share of gold deposits jumped to 6.4 percent – almost back to the 2001 level.

The RBI is likely to persist with its strategy of investing its reserves mainly in liquid assets (US dollars, Euro deposits and bonds), but with a conscious decision to further reduce concentration in US dollar-denominated assets when the opportunity arises, by purchasing commodities such as gold. But how aggressively they do so remains to be seen.

# 20

# The Importance of Remittances in India and South Asia[1]

*(with Sasidaran Gopalan)*

Despite the notable improvements in the economic climates and growth prospects of many developing economies in Asia, poverty remains a complex and persistent issue confronting policymakers. Poverty estimates published by the World Bank in 2008 reveal that in 2005 nearly 1.4 billion people in the developing world were living on less than USD 1.25 a day.[2] While acknowledging that there has been considerable progress in reducing poverty levels – the corresponding numbers in absolute poverty were about 1.9 billion in 1981 – much remains to be done to ensure that the benefits of economic growth are more evenly distributed, in order to eradicate poverty worldwide.

Recognising the importance of effective and immediate policy action to reduce poverty in developing countries, concerted steps have been taken at the multilateral, regional and country level towards this goal, of which the United Nations Millennium Development Goals (MDGs) have been a key initiative. An area that requires more attention, however, is that of the resource constraints that have constantly plagued this and similar poverty alleviation efforts.

While there are clearly many sources of internal finance that could and should be tapped (by streamlining government finances, improving domestic financial intermediation, the use of foreign exchange reserves, and the like), developing countries will inevitably have to supplement these with external sources of finance to achieve their anti-poverty and pro-development goals.

Most developing countries depend heavily on official sources of external financing such as grants and concessionary loans, often referred to as Official Development Assistance (ODA). ODA, which includes debt relief as one of its vital components, is especially important for many of the poorest countries burdened by heavy debt service payments. However, in light of decreasing net ODA disbursements (including debt relief) from donor countries in the recent years, it has become essential to consider other types of private sources of external financing that could help these developing countries realise their development goals.

World Bank data on net resource flows to the developing economies on the whole reveal that net total private capital flows, including workers' remittances, to all developing countries peaked just before the Asian financial crisis in 1997, dipped during the crisis, and has been on a gradual recovery since. Net total private flows, including workers' remittances, to all developing countries in 2007 surpassed USD 1,420 billion compared to about USD 270–290 billion in 2000–02 (Table 20.1).

Net FDI inflows and workers' remittances clearly emerge as the most significant components of external financing for the developing countries. Over the 2000–07 period, on average, about three quarters of the total private inflows into the developing countries comprised FDI and workers' remittances. The remaining two components of external financing are foreign portfolio equity inflows and short-term debt inflows. While net portfolio equity inflows have risen more than ten-fold rise since 2000, increasing from about USD 13.5 billion in

*Table 20.1* Components of private external financing in developing countries (billions of USD)

| Year | Workers' remittances | Net FDI inflows | Net portfolio equity inflows | Net short-term debt flows | Net total private inflows (incl. remittances) |
|---|---|---|---|---|---|
| 2000 | 84.5 | 165.5 | 13.5 | −6.4 | 271.5 |
| 2001 | 95.6 | 166 | 6.3 | 22.9 | 292.9 |
| 2002 | 115.9 | 152.5 | 9 | −5.4 | 272.7 |
| 2003 | 143.6 | 155.5 | 25.5 | 61.5 | 412.7 |
| 2004 | 161.3 | 216 | 38.7 | 68.5 | 557.8 |
| 2005 | 191.2 | 279.1 | 68.1 | 86.6 | 760.9 |
| 2006 | 229 | 358.4 | 104.3 | 110.1 | 968.2 |
| 2007 | 265 | 520 | 138.6 | 202.5 | 1422.5 |

*Source*: Based on World Bank (2009). *Global Development Finance 2009*, World Bank: Washington DC.

2000 to USD 139 billion in 2007, net short-term debt flows witnessed an even more dramatic increase, from about USD 3 billion in the year 2002 to nearly USD 203 billion in 2007. However, both these components tend to be highly variable and hence might be considered rather unstable sources of financing (an issue discussed later in this chapter).

Workers' remittances alone have constituted one-third of the net total private capital flows into the developing countries, second only to FDI flows. Despite this, somewhat less attention has been paid to this source of financing. Available data from the World Bank shows that there has been a marked increase in the volume of workers' remittances to the developing countries, from about USD 85 billion in 2000 to about USD 280 billion in 2007, and the total is estimated to have exceeded USD 300 billion in 2008.[3] Among the developing countries, South Asia received, on average, about 20 percent of global remittance receipts destined for the developing countries between 2000 and 2007.

It is interesting to observe that remittance inflows to this region have actually remained quite resilient, even during the GFC. It is well known that South Asia, like most other emerging economies, experienced sharp net capital outflows following the crisis. According to available estimates from the World Bank, net private capital inflows almost halved from USD 112 billion in 2007 to USD 66 billion in 2008. In contrast, remittance flows to South Asia actually remained stable with a slight upward trend, rising from USD 52 billion in 2007 to an estimated USD 66 billion in 2008, the same as total net private capital inflows to the region.[4] Given the significance of remittance inflows to individual South Asian economies, we consider this component in more detail below.

As Table 20.2 shows, the lion's share of the inflows has gone to India over the years (about 70 percent). The average remittance inflows to India between 1995 and 2007 stood at about USD 16 billion. For the corresponding period, the average inflows to Bangladesh and Pakistan were about USD 2.7–2.8 billion, while those to Sri Lanka were about half that, at USD 1.4 billion.

While the absolute values indicate India's dominance as a host of South Asian remittance flows, this is not surprising in view of the fact that India constitutes about 80 percent of aggregate South Asian output. Referring to Table 20.2 again, it is clear that in 2007, Bangladesh had the highest share of remittances as a percentage of its GDP (10 percent), followed closely by Sri Lanka (8 percent).[5] Pakistan and India lag with shares of 4 and 3 percent, respectively. While Bangladesh has

*Table 20.2* Significance of remittances in select South Asian economies

| | Bangladesh | | Pakistan | | India | | Sri Lanka | |
|---|---|---|---|---|---|---|---|---|
| Year | Workers' remittances (USD billions) | Percent of GDP | Workers' remittances (USD billions) | Percent of GDP | Workers' remittances (USD billions) | Percent of GDP | Workers' remittances (USD billions) | Percent of GDP |
| 1995 | 1.20 | 3.17 | 1.71 | 2.82 | 6.22 | 1.75 | 0.81 | 6.21 |
| 1996 | 1.35 | 3.31 | 1.28 | 2.03 | 8.77 | 2.26 | 0.85 | 6.13 |
| 1997 | 1.53 | 3.61 | 1.71 | 2.73 | 10.33 | 2.51 | 0.94 | 6.24 |
| 1998 | 1.61 | 3.64 | 1.17 | 1.88 | 9.48 | 2.28 | 1.02 | 6.48 |
| 1999 | 1.81 | 3.95 | 1.00 | 1.58 | 11.12 | 2.47 | 1.07 | 6.85 |
| 2000 | 1.97 | 4.18 | 1.08 | 1.45 | 12.89 | 2.80 | 1.17 | 7.14 |
| 2001 | 2.11 | 4.48 | 1.46 | 2.02 | 14.27 | 2.99 | 1.19 | 7.53 |
| 2002 | 2.86 | 6.01 | 3.55 | 4.92 | 15.74 | 3.10 | 1.31 | 7.65 |
| 2003 | 3.19 | 6.15 | 3.96 | 4.76 | 21.00 | 3.50 | 1.44 | 7.62 |
| 2004 | 3.58 | 6.34 | 3.95 | 4.03 | 18.75 | 2.68 | 1.59 | 7.69 |
| 2005 | 4.31 | 7.16 | 4.28 | 3.91 | 21.29 | 2.63 | 1.99 | 8.16 |
| 2006 | 5.43 | 8.77 | 5.12 | 4.02 | 25.43 | 2.78 | 2.18 | 7.73 |
| 2007 | 6.56 | 9.59 | 6.00 | 4.20 | 35.26 | 3.29 | 2.53 | 7.81 |

*Source*: Compiled from World Development Indicators Online, The World Bank.

experienced a steady rise in remittance inflows as a share of GDP, there appears to be no obvious pattern in the shares of other countries.

Another useful indicator that underlines the significance of remittances to these economies is the share it represents of total external private sources of financing. The average share (over the period 1995–2007) of remittance inflows, expressed as a percentage of the sum of total private capital flows, stands at about 25 percent for Bangladesh, the corresponding figures for the other three South Asian countries being about 15–17 percent (Table 20.3). Clearly workers' remittances are an important source of external financing in absolute and relative terms for the South Asian economies, especially Bangladesh.

After decades of neglect, workers' remittances have become recognised by policymakers and observers as important sources of external finance. There is, in fact, a growing body of literature that deals with this issue.[6] One of the most important features of the remittances component is the stability of such flows in contrast to other types of private capital flows. A simple way to examine the relative volatilities over a short period is to compute the coefficient of variations (CVs) of the various sources of financing.[7] We compute CVs for the individual South Asian countries over a period of 12 years from 1995 to 2007.[8]

Figure 20.1 reveals the volatilities of the various sources of financing for the individual South Asian countries. The CVs corroborate our earlier point about workers' remittances being more stable than the other sources of external finance, followed by trade flows and FDI flows. As expected, foreign portfolio flows and short-term commercial bank lending appear to be the most volatile components in all countries. It is not without reason that these components are referred to as "mobile capital". Computing such CVs for all the developing countries lumped together produces broadly similar results.

Beyond this measure of volatility, arguably of more importance is the fact that while private capital flows are generally considered *pro-cyclical*, i.e. capital flows increase during growth booms and fall during busts, remittances are generally expected to be *counter-cyclical*. Thus, remittances could serve as macroeconomic stabilisers during times of an economic slowdown, as migrants are expected to increase the amounts of money they remit back home when most needed (i.e. during a downturn in their home country).[9] As a significant portion of migrants' incomes is being spent in home countries, this could also provide the much-needed economic stimulus to domestic demand in times of economic distress. Also, in contrast to other types of capital flows, workers' remittances do not create future liabilities, such as debt servicing.[10]

*Table 20.3* Total private sources of external financing in South Asia and relative share of remittances

| | Bangladesh | | Pakistan | | India | | Sri Lanka | |
|---|---|---|---|---|---|---|---|---|
| Year | Total private external financing (USD billions) | Remittances as a percentage of total private financing | Total private external financing (USD billions) | Remittances as a percentage of total private financing | Total private external financing (USD billions) | Remittances as a percentage of total private financing | Total private external financing (USD billions) | Remittances as a percentage of total private financing |
| 1995 | 5.60 | 21.47 | 12.97 | 13.19 | 48.82 | 12.75 | 5.59 | 14.48 |
| 1996 | 5.83 | 23.09 | 13.40 | 9.58 | 55.92 | 15.68 | 5.90 | 14.44 |
| 1997 | 7.15 | 21.34 | 13.59 | 12.56 | 60.38 | 17.11 | 7.06 | 13.35 |
| 1998 | 7.63 | 21.06 | 11.23 | 10.44 | 56.29 | 16.84 | 7.11 | 14.39 |
| 1999 | 8.21 | 22.01 | 10.22 | 9.75 | 66.53 | 16.72 | 6.73 | 15.94 |
| 2000 | 9.50 | 20.72 | 11.17 | 9.63 | 76.87 | 16.77 | 7.92 | 14.73 |
| 2001 | 9.25 | 22.76 | 11.74 | 12.45 | 82.28 | 17.35 | 7.39 | 16.04 |
| 2002 | 9.94 | 28.75 | 16.31 | 21.78 | 92.56 | 17.00 | 7.36 | 17.78 |
| 2003 | 11.50 | 27.75 | 18.84 | 21.04 | 121.31 | 17.31 | 8.06 | 17.84 |
| 2004 | 13.25 | 27.05 | 20.99 | 18.79 | 148.57 | 12.62 | 8.94 | 17.77 |
| 2005 | 15.68 | 27.51 | 25.66 | 16.68 | 199.96 | 10.65 | 9.90 | 20.11 |
| 2006 | 19.02 | 28.54 | 30.75 | 16.66 | 257.98 | 9.86 | 10.87 | 20.09 |
| 2007 | 21.44 | 30.61 | 34.14 | 17.57 | 87.95 | 40.09 | 12.49 | 20.23 |

*Note*: Components of private sources of external financing – exports of goods and services, net FDI inflows, worker remittances, net portfolio equity inflows, commercial banks and other lending.
*Source*: Compiled from World Development Indicators Online, The World Bank.

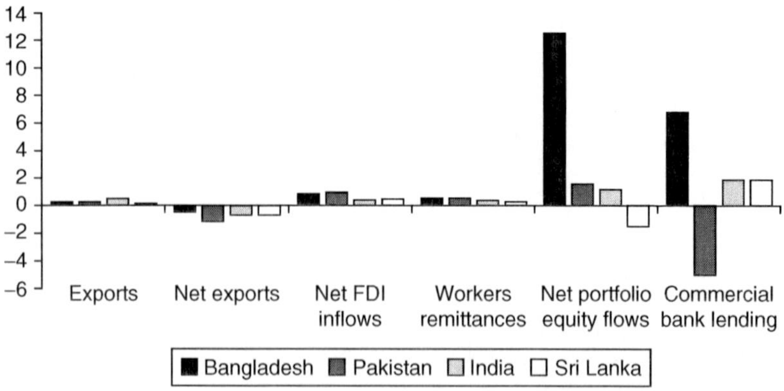


*Figure 20.1* Volatility of components of private external financing in select South Asian countries, 1995–2007

*Source*: Author's calculations based on World Development Indicators Online, The World Bank.

Overall, workers' remittances are potentially the most stable and vital source of financing for developing countries, especially to South Asia. An important policy area of concern that needs to be addressed by all affected countries is the presence of excessively high transaction costs associated with remittance transfers. Some estimates indicate that remittance service providers in the formal sector charge a remittance fee that is 10–15 percent higher than the principal amount, which typically leads to a reduction in the amount of net funds transferred. Effective bilateral cooperation arrangements between the remittance-originating countries and the remittance-recipient countries could prove to be useful in reducing such high transaction costs. Apart from the huge financial burden that is placed on the remitters, the presence of high transaction costs has also resulted in the growth of informal channels of remittances. This implies that workers' remittances are in reality much more significant than the official numbers suggest.

In the final analysis, while remittances have become significant private financial resources for households in developing countries, they cannot be considered as a substitute for other sources of development financing like the FDI, which might generate broader multiplier effects on the economy. Countries should therefore work towards mobilising a range of international resources to meet their development objectives.

# Part V

# Foreign Direct Investment Issues in Asia

# 21

# Foreign Portfolio versus Foreign Direct Investment Flows: Are They So Different?[1]

Many emerging economies in Asia and elsewhere have been faced with sharply volatile capital flows, mainly driven by sharp booms and busts in foreign portfolio and short-term bank flows, together referred to as "mobile capital". In contrast, FDI flows have remained remarkably stable (see Chapter 20). The policy focus on this "mobile capital" has tried to limit such flows via capital account restrictions or through prudential measures, or by ensuring that the central bank holds enough low-yielding liquid assets (i.e. foreign exchange reserves) to cover possible sudden withdrawals.

There are many currency crisis models that conveniently explain the volatility of short-term capital flows, covering both bank lending and portfolio flows. The essence of these models is that a relatively small initial loss of confidence can quickly translate into panic and a mass exodus of funds, especially when international reserves fall below a threshold where they become insufficient to cover short-term liabilities, making a country vulnerable to crisis. In contrast, FDI is determined by long-term fundamental economic characteristics, which are more stable. Indeed, FDI is often presented as being relatively irreversible in the short-run. Since it is supposed to enhance the productive capacity of the host country, it produces the revenue stream necessary to cover future capital outflows. The above theory, combined with the empirical evidence for developing countries, has resulted in the conventional wisdom that switching from short-term to long-term capital flows may reduce the probability of currency crises.

But is the conventional wisdom unassailable? A potential criticism of the conventional view regarding differing degrees of stability of various capital flows is that it fails to take into account the complex interactions between FDI and other flows. Examining each flow individually, particularly during short periods of time (such as year-to-year variations), may be an unreliable indicator of the degree of risk of various classes of flow, and could even be highly misleading. Capital that flows in under the guise of FDI could flow out under another guise. Contrary to popular belief, FDI is not quite "bolted down", although the physical assets it finances are. Foreign investors can use the physical assets as collateral to obtain loans from banks, and can then place the funds abroad. In other words, the foreign direct investor may hedge the firm's FDI exposure by borrowing domestically and then taking short-term capital out of the country. Hence, a firm may be doing one thing with its assets and a completely different thing with the manner in which it finances them.

It is true that the distinction between foreign equity portfolio and FDI flows in the balance of payments can be somewhat arbitrary. Small differences in equity ownership, which may serve to reclassify financial flows, are unlikely to represent substantially different investment horizons. This is especially relevant in view of the fact that an increasing share of FDI in recent years is in the form of mergers and acquisitions (M&As – i.e. an ownership stake of over 10 percent) as opposed to green field investments (Figure 21.1). M&As are also the usual reason for an increase in FDI immediately after a crisis as foreign investors purchase assets in fire sales.[2] The growing significance of M&As is an important

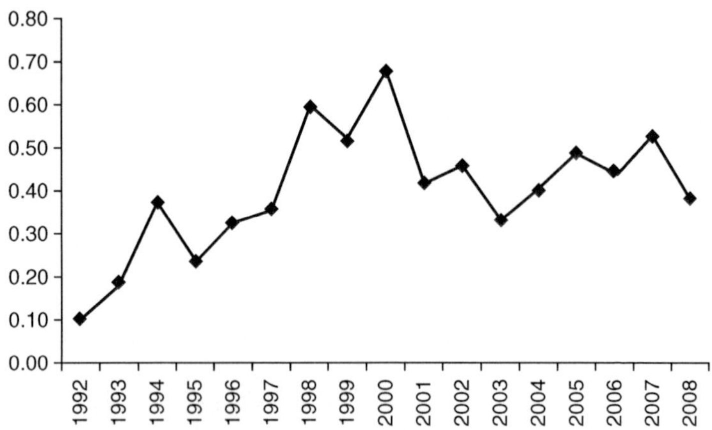


*Figure 21.1* Ratio of global M&A to FDI, 1992–2008

*Source*: UNCTAD (2008). *World Investment Report 2008*. UN, New York and Geneva.

but often overlooked point. If a foreign entity undertakes a cross-border acquisition of less than 10 percent, it is regarded as a FPI flow, as, for example, when the Chinese sovereign wealth fund (SWF) purchased an initial 9.9 percent stake in the largest US private equity firm, Blackstone Group. Therefore, this investment enters the balance of payments as an FPI flow from China to the US. If the Chinese had purchased a stake of more than 10 percent, the transaction would have been categorised as FDI. This and other investments by foreign SWFs in the US have tended in recent times to be less than 10 percent so that they are not categorised as FDI and therefore do not need to undergo the evaluation by Committee on Foreign Investment in the United States (CFIUS).[3]

Given this marginal difference between them, it is rather curious to expect the two categories of investment flow to be such different beasts. Do small differences in equity ownership represent substantially different investment horizons? A potential danger is that policy measures designed to encourage FDI may involve not only a distortionary cost but also little gain in terms of enhanced financial stability. Given the intricate interconnections between FDI and "mobile capital", there is clearly a need for a deeper analysis of this issue.

# 22
# Intra-Asian Foreign Direct Investment Flows[1]

*(with Rabin Hattari)*

According to UNCTAD, "a number of developing countries have emerged as significant sources of FDI in other developing countries, and their investments are now considered a new and important source of capital and production know-how, especially for host countries in developing regions."[2] The phenomenon of South-South FDI flows, particularly those arising from multinational corporations (MNCs) in China and India, has generated significant interest from policymakers, academia and the popular press in recent times.

Available data from the Word Bank indicates that South-South FDI has increased almost three-fold (from USD 14 billion in 1995 to USD 47 billion in 2003) and accounts for almost 37 percent of total FDI flows to developing countries, up from 15 percent in 1995.[3] The Chinese government has stated its intention to help develop 30–50 "national champions" that can "go global" in the near term.[4] Given this, along with aggressive overseas acquisition plans by cash-rich and highly confident firms from India, Hong Kong, South Korea and Taiwan, as well as by national holding companies in Singapore (Temasek Holdings) and Malaysia (Khazana National Berhad), outward investments by Asian companies are set to rise further.

Apart from the usual efficiency-seeking, resource-seeking and market-seeking investments, outward FDI (OFDI) from developing Asia is motivated by a desire to build a global presence and buy brand names, technology, processes, management know-how and marketing and distribution networks. The international expansion of some Asian firms may also have been motivated by a desire to offset or diversify risks at home, for tariff-jumping reasons, geopolitical factors, etc. Policymakers in many Asian countries such as China and India have been particularly keen on promoting an internationalising thrust and have facilitated

OFDI via the gradual liberalisation of rules governing capital account outflows and, in many cases, providing a financing mechanism to domestic firms looking to invest abroad.

While Asian companies have become significant foreign direct investors abroad, a large share of outward investments from Asia may have been recycled intraregionally. According to some rough estimates, intra-Asian FDI flows in 2004 accounted for about 40 percent of Asia's total FDI inflows.[5] If correct, this share is broadly comparable to the extent of intra-Asian trade flows. However, unlike trade flows, there has been little to no detailed examination of FDI flows between Asian economies at a bilateral level.

The Triad (the EU, Japan and the United States) continue to dominate both as sources and hosts of FDI in terms of both stocks and flows (Table 22.1). However, it is interesting to note that in 2003–2005 the Triad's share of FDI flows declined to a low of below 60 percent compared to about 80 percent on average between 1978 and 1990, while that to developing economies rose to a corresponding high of 40 percent, over half of which was destined for Asia. The share of FDI outflows from developing economies, negligible until the mid-1980s, rose to about 15 percent of world outflows in 2005.

Table 22.2 focuses specifically on the FDI inflows and outflows of selected Asian developing economies between 1990 and 2005. Between 1990 and 1996, FDI inflows to Asia grew at an average annual rate of just over USD 50 billion, while outflows grew at a rate of USD 30 billion during the same period. Buoyant global economic conditions and the liberalisation of most of the Asian economies in the early 1990s led to a rise in inflows to the region. In contrast, during 1997–2005, average annual FDI growth in outflows from Asia outpaced inflows to Asia (USD 22 billion on average compared with USD 50 billion annually).

Interestingly, the two countries with the largest inflows and outflows are China and Hong Kong. In both of our sample periods (1990–1996 and 1997–2005), China has been the single largest host of FDI, contributing between 38 and 40 percent of inflows to developing Asia during the last 15 years. With regard to outflows, Hong Kong is clearly the single largest source of FDI outflows from Asia. FDI outflows from Hong Kong averaged just under USD 15 billion annually in the first sub-period and over USD 25 billion in the second sub-period. As will be noted later, a large part of outflows from Hong Kong is bound for China, some of which is due to round-tripping from the Chinese Mainland to begin with. This round-tripping significantly inflates the amount of OFDI from the Mainland, which itself experienced a spurt between 1990 and 2005.

*Table 22.1* Distribution of FDI by region and selected countries, 1980–2005 (in percentages)

| | Inward stock | | | | Outward stock | | | |
|---|---|---|---|---|---|---|---|---|
| **Region** | **1980** | **1990** | **2000** | **2005** | **1980** | **1990** | **2000** | **2005** |
| Developed economies | 75.6 | 79.3 | 68.5 | 70.3 | 87.3 | 91.7 | 86.2 | 86.9 |
| European Union | 42.5 | 42.9 | 37.6 | 44.4 | 37.2 | 45.2 | 47.1 | 51.3 |
| Japan | 0.6 | 0.6 | 0.9 | 1.0 | 3.4 | 11.2 | 4.3 | 3.6 |
| United States | 14.8 | 22.1 | 21.7 | 16.0 | 37.7 | 24.0 | 20.3 | 19.2 |
| Developing economies | 24.4 | 20.7 | 30.3 | 27.2 | 12.7 | 8.3 | 13.5 | 11.9 |
| Africa | 6.9 | 3.3 | 2.6 | 2.6 | 1.3 | 1.1 | 0.7 | 0.5 |
| Latin America and the Caribbean | 7.1 | 6.6 | 9.3 | 9.3 | 6.5 | 3.4 | 3.3 | 3.2 |
| Asia | 10.5 | 10.8 | 18.4 | 15.4 | 2.9 | 3.8 | 9.5 | 8.2 |
| West Asia | 1.4 | 2.2 | 1.1 | 1.5 | 0.3 | 0.4 | 0.2 | 0.3 |
| South, East and Southeast Asia | 8.8 | 8.5 | 17.2 | 13.8 | 2.5 | 3.4 | 9.3 | 7.6 |
| South-East Europe and CIS | – | 0.01 | 1.2 | 2.5 | – | 0.01 | 0.3 | 1.2 |
| World | 100.0 | 100.0 | 100.0 | 100.0 | 100.0 | 100.0 | 100.0 | 100.0 |
| | **Inflow** | | | | **Outflow** | | | |
| **Region** | **1978–1980** | **1988–1990** | **1998–2000** | **2003–2005** | **1978–1980** | **1988–1990** | **1998–2000** | **2003–2005** |
| Developed economies | 79.7 | 82.5 | 77.3 | 59.4 | 97.0 | 93.1 | 90.4 | 85.8 |
| European Union | 39.1 | 40.3 | 46.0 | 40.7 | 44.8 | 50.6 | 64.4 | 54.6 |
| Japan | 0.4 | 0.04 | 0.8 | 0.8 | 4.9 | 19.7 | 2.6 | 4.9 |
| United States | 23.8 | 31.5 | 24.0 | 12.5 | 39.7 | 13.6 | 15.9 | 15.7 |
| Developing economies | 20.3 | 17.5 | 21.7 | 35.9 | 3.0 | 6.9 | 9.4 | 12.3 |
| Africa | 2.0 | 1.9 | 1.0 | 3.0 | 1.0 | 0.4 | 0.2 | 0.2 |
| Latin America and the Caribbean | 13.0 | 5.0 | 9.7 | 11.5 | 1.1 | 1.0 | 4.1 | 3.5 |
| Asia | 5.3 | 10.5 | 11.0 | 21.4 | 0.9 | 5.6 | 5.1 | 8.6 |
| West Asia | –1.6 | 0.3 | 0.3 | 3.0 | 0.3 | 0.5 | 0.1 | 1.0 |
| South, East and Southeast Asia | 6.7 | 10.0 | 10.7 | 18.4 | 0.6 | 5.1 | 5.0 | 7.7 |
| South-East Europe and CIS | 0.0 | 0.02 | 0.9 | 4.7 | – | 0.01 | 0.2 | 1.8 |
| World | 100.0 | 100.0 | 99.9 | 100.0 | 100.0 | 100.0 | 100.0 | 100.0 |

*Source*: UNCTAD FDI/TNC database.

Excluding Hong Kong from the analysis, the picture is more even across our sample countries. It is apparent that the three NIEs of Singapore, South Korea and Taiwan have consistently remained among the top developing economy sources of FDI over the last two decades. Malaysia (a near-NIE) is also notable for the size of their OFDI flows, particularly since the 1990s. Indonesia remains an important source of FDI, while more aggressive internationalisation strategies by Indian companies has seen it rise in rankings from 39 in 1990 to the top 20 by 2005. These seven economies constitute the bulk of OFDI from Asia.

Having considered broad country aggregate outflows and inflows from and to Asia, we analyse bilateral FDI between Asian economies. This exercise is far from straightforward. UNCTAD data on inflows and outflows do not match exactly. It is apparent that UNCTAD FDI data on outflows from source countries are incomplete for many countries. While some source countries have relatively complete outflows data, others either have incomplete data or none at all. Different reporting practices of FDI data create bilateral discrepancies between the FDI flows reported by home and host countries, and the differences can be quite large. Faced with these concerns we draw inferences about FDI outflows by examining FDI inflow data reported in the host economies, as they are more complete and are available for all developing Asian economies under consideration. In other words, we focus on the *sources of inflows* rather than the *host of outflows*. To keep the analysis manageable we examine data for the averages of 1997–2000, and 2001–2005, rather than on an annual basis.

FDI inflows between Asian countries account for about one-third of all FDI inflows to the region and are particularly pronounced between and within East Asian economies and Southeast Asian economies. The average of FDI flows from Hong Kong to China and vice versa from 1997 to 2005 has been around USD 24 billion, and accounts for almost of 40 percent of intra-Asia flows. Apart from Hong Kong-China-Taiwan flows, bilateral flows between East and Southeast Asia are also significant (Table 22.3). Almost three-fifths of flows from East Asia to Southeast Asia have been destined for the higher-income Southeast economies, i.e. Singapore, Malaysia, the Philippines and Thailand. Singapore has attracted about half of all East Asian FDI destined for Southeast Asia, and has also been a major investor in China. Malaysia and Thailand have also invested in China.

Consideration of intra-Asian bilateral flows highlights a few other important characteristics of intra-Asian FDI flows. First, the leading investors from the region have stayed the same from 1997 to 2006, with Hong Kong as the leader, followed by Singapore, Taiwan, South

*Table 22.2* FDI inflows and outflows of selected Asian countries (in billions of US dollars)

| Country | 1990–1996 | 1997–2005 | 1997 | 1998 | 1999 | 2000 | 2001 | 2002 | 2003 | 2004 | 2005 |
|---|---|---|---|---|---|---|---|---|---|---|---|
| **Inflows** | | | | | | | | | | | |
| *World* | *248.30* | *816.23* | *489.71* | *712.03* | *1,099.92* | *1,409.57* | *832.25* | *617.73* | *557.87* | *710.75* | *916.28* |
| *Asia (excluding Japan)* | *51.31* | *114.56* | *100.40* | *91.06* | *108.66* | *143.83* | *103.99* | *88.61* | *93.72* | *137.02* | *163.72* |
| *New Industrial Asia* | *9.18* | *21.55* | *18.64* | *12.60* | *29.13* | *30.06* | *23.62* | *11.83* | *14.72* | *24.45* | *28.91* |
| Korea | 2.34 | 5.75 | 2.64 | 5.07 | 9.63 | 8.65 | 3.87 | 3.04 | 3.89 | 7.73 | 7.20 |
| Singapore | 5.89 | 13.60 | 13.75 | 7.31 | 16.58 | 16.48 | 15.65 | 7.34 | 10.38 | 14.82 | 20.08 |
| Taiwan POC | 0.95 | 2.21 | 2.25 | 0.22 | 2.93 | 4.93 | 4.11 | 1.45 | 0.45 | 1.90 | 1.63 |
| *China* | *25.00* | *76.40* | *56.63* | *60.23* | *64.90* | *102.64* | *70.65* | *62.42* | *67.13* | *94.66* | *108.30* |
| China: Mainland | 20.43 | 50.88 | 45.26 | 45.46 | 40.32 | 40.71 | 46.88 | 52.74 | 53.51 | 60.63 | 72.41 |
| Hong Kong | 4.57 | 25.52 | 11.37 | 14.76 | 24.58 | 61.92 | 23.78 | 9.68 | 13.62 | 34.03 | 35.90 |
| *ASEAN-4* | *8.48* | *8.50* | *16.13* | *11.72* | *9.37* | *4.83* | *1.66* | *5.84* | *4.32* | *8.62* | *14.05* |
| Indonesia | 2.71 | 0.19 | 4.68 | –0.24 | –1.87 | –4.55 | –2.98 | 0.15 | –0.60 | 1.90 | 5.26 |
| Malaysia | 3.62 | 3.50 | 6.32 | 2.71 | 3.90 | 3.79 | 0.55 | 3.20 | 2.47 | 4.62 | 3.97 |
| Philippines | 0.92 | 1.17 | 1.25 | 1.75 | 1.25 | 2.24 | 0.20 | 1.54 | 0.49 | 0.69 | 1.13 |
| Thailand | 1.23 | 3.63 | 3.88 | 7.49 | 6.09 | 3.35 | 3.89 | 0.95 | 1.95 | 1.41 | 3.69 |
| *South Asia* | *2.44* | *5.90* | *5.34* | *3.87* | *3.21* | *4.65* | *6.38* | *6.97* | *5.70* | *7.29* | *9.75* |
| India | 1.38 | 4.42 | 3.62 | 2.63 | 2.17 | 3.59 | 5.47 | 5.63 | 4.59 | 5.47 | 6.60 |
| Pakistan | 0.34 | 0.79 | 0.71 | 0.51 | 0.53 | 0.31 | 0.38 | 0.82 | 0.53 | 1.12 | 2.18 |
| Sri Lanka | 0.09 | 0.23 | 0.43 | 0.15 | 0.20 | 0.17 | 0.17 | 0.20 | 0.23 | 0.23 | 0.27 |
| Bangladesh | 0.63 | 0.47 | 0.58 | 0.58 | 0.31 | 0.58 | 0.35 | 0.33 | 0.35 | 0.46 | 0.69 |

**Outflows**

| | | | | | | | | | | | |
|---|---|---|---|---|---|---|---|---|---|---|---|
| *World* | *269.72* | *776.31* | *483.14* | *694.40* | *1,108.17* | *1,244.47* | *764.20* | *539.54* | *561.10* | *813.07* | *778.73* |
| *Asia (excluding Japan)* | *29.14* | *50.05* | *51.23* | *31.69* | *39.87* | *80.69* | *48.35* | *33.76* | *21.15* | *76.11* | *67.63* |
| *New Industrial Asia* | *8.92* | *16.87* | *20.60* | *10.74* | *16.62* | *17.62* | *28.07* | *9.79* | *12.25* | *20.32* | *15.86* |
| Korea | 2.25 | 3.98 | 4.45 | 4.74 | 4.20 | 5.00 | 2.42 | 2.62 | 3.43 | 4.66 | 4.31 |
| Singapore | 3.62 | 7.40 | 10.90 | 2.16 | 8.00 | 5.92 | 20.17 | 2.29 | 3.14 | 8.51 | 5.52 |
| Taiwan POC | 3.05 | 5.49 | 5.24 | 3.84 | 4.42 | 6.70 | 5.48 | 4.89 | 5.68 | 7.15 | 6.03 |
| China | 17.21 | 29.22 | 26.97 | 19.62 | 21.14 | 60.27 | 18.23 | 19.98 | 5.34 | 47.52 | 43.87 |
| China: Mainland | 2.32 | 3.36 | 2.56 | 2.63 | 1.77 | 0.92 | 6.89 | 2.52 | −0.15 | 1.81 | 11.31 |
| Hong Kong | 14.89 | 25.85 | 24.41 | 16.98 | 19.37 | 59.35 | 11.35 | 17.46 | 5.49 | 45.72 | 32.56 |
| *ASEAN-4* | *2.94* | *2.96* | *3.57* | *1.20* | *1.98* | *2.28* | *0.60* | *2.26* | *2.17* | *6.17* | *6.44* |
| Indonesia | 0.91 | 0.80 | 0.18 | 0.04 | 0.07 | 0.15 | 0.13 | 0.18 | 0.01 | 3.41 | 3.07 |
| Malaysia | 1.44 | 1.73 | 2.68 | 0.86 | 1.42 | 2.03 | 0.27 | 1.90 | 1.37 | 2.06 | 2.97 |
| Philippines | 0.16 | 0.17 | 0.14 | 0.16 | 0.13 | 0.13 | −0.14 | 0.07 | 0.30 | 0.58 | 0.16 |
| Thailand | 0.43 | 0.26 | 0.58 | 0.13 | 0.35 | −0.02 | 0.35 | 0.11 | 0.49 | 0.13 | 0.25 |
| *South Asia* | *0.07* | *1.00* | *0.10* | *0.11* | *0.13* | *0.52* | *1.45* | *1.72* | *1.38* | *2.09* | *1.46* |
| India | 0.07 | 0.95 | 0.11 | 0.05 | 0.08 | 0.51 | 1.40 | 1.68 | 1.33 | 2.02 | 1.36 |
| Pakistan | 0.00 | 0.03 | −0.02 | 0.05 | 0.02 | 0.01 | 0.03 | 0.03 | 0.02 | 0.06 | 0.04 |
| Sri Lanka | 0.00 | 0.01 | 0.01 | 0.01 | 0.02 | 0.00 | 0.00 | 0.01 | 0.03 | 0.01 | 0.04 |
| Bangladesh | 0.00 | 0.01 | 0.00 | 0.00 | 0.00 | 0.00 | 0.02 | 0.00 | 0.01 | 0.01 | 0.01 |

*Source*: UNCTAD FDI/TNC database.

*Table 22.3* Top 50 bilateral flows between Asian countries*

| | | Average (USD millions) | | In percent to Asia | |
|---|---|---|---|---|---|
| **Source** | **Host** | **(1997–00)** | **(2001–05)** | **(1997–00)** | **(2001–05)** |
| Hong Kong | China | 17750.8 | 17819.1 | 46.2 | 50.7 |
| China | Hong Kong | 7266.9 | 5459.4 | 18.9 | 15.5 |
| Singapore | China | 2706.3 | 2136.7 | 7 | 6.1 |
| Singapore | Hong Kong | 2835.3 | 353.1 | 7.4 | 1 |
| Singapore | Malaysia | 844.1 | 1133.8 | 2.2 | 3.2 |
| Singapore | Thailand | 441.7 | 1381.9 | 1.1 | 3.9 |
| Malaysia | China | 290.8 | 316.7 | 0.8 | 0.9 |
| Hong Kong | Malaysia | 272.3 | 296.5 | 0.7 | 0.8 |
| Hong Kong | Thailand | 360.1 | 160.8 | 0.9 | 0.5 |
| South Korea | Hong Kong | 313 | 155.7 | 0.8 | 0.4 |
| Thailand | China | 185.8 | 183.7 | 0.5 | 0.5 |
| Philippines | China | 135.9 | 212.2 | 0.4 | 0.6 |
| Hong Kong | Singapore | 250.1 | 81.9 | 0.7 | 0.2 |
| Malaysia | Hong Kong | 62 | 147.2 | 0.2 | 0.4 |
| Singapore | Philippines | 88.9 | 76.1 | 0.2 | 0.2 |
| Hong Kong | South Korea | 79.2 | 51.5 | 0.2 | 0.1 |
| Thailand | Hong Kong | –3.1 | 110.7 | 0 | 0.3 |
| Hong Kong | Philippines | 50 | 54.4 | 0.1 | 0.2 |
| Singapore | India | 22 | 67.6 | 0.1 | 0.2 |
| China | Singapore | –17.3 | 99.9 | 0 | 0.3 |
| China | Philippines | 71.8 | –0.1 | 0.2 | 0 |
| India | Singapore | 36.8 | 24.9 | 0.1 | 0.1 |
| Philippines | Thailand | 4.9 | 48.4 | 0 | 0.1 |
| China | Cambodia | 18.3 | 33.4 | 0 | 0.1 |
| Malaysia | Cambodia | 24.9 | 16.7 | 0.1 | 0 |
| Malaysia | Thailand | 19.4 | 21.2 | 0.1 | 0.1 |
| Singapore | Cambodia | 19.6 | 12.9 | 0.1 | 0 |
| Thailand | Cambodia | 19.1 | 13.4 | 0 | 0 |
| Philippines | Malaysia | 6.3 | 18.7 | 0 | 0.1 |
| Malaysia | Bangladesh | 5.1 | 19.4 | 0 | 0.1 |
| Philippines | Singapore | 37.5 | –15.6 | 0.1 | 0 |
| Thailand | Malaysia | 10.2 | 11.1 | 0 | 0 |
| Malaysia | Lao PDR | 17.4 | 0.9 | 0 | 0 |
| Thailand | Lao PDR | 15.2 | 1.9 | 0 | 0 |
| China | Malaysia | 11.5 | 5.1 | 0 | 0 |
| Pakistan | Bangladesh | 1.3 | 10.7 | 0 | 0 |
| China | Thailand | 0.4 | 10.8 | 0 | 0 |
| China | Lao PDR | 3.9 | 6.6 | 0 | 0 |
| Malaysia | Philippines | 6.5 | 2.4 | 0 | 0 |
| Singapore | Myanmar | 0 | 8.7 | 0 | 0 |
| Thailand | Myanmar | 0 | 5.6 | 0 | 0 |

Continued

*Table 22.3* Continued

| | | Average (USD millions) | | In percent to Asia | |
|---|---|---|---|---|---|
| **Source** | **Host** | **(1997–00)** | **(2001–05)** | **(1997–00)** | **(2001–05)** |
| Myanmar | Singapore | 4.1 | 1.1 | 0 | 0 |
| China | Myanmar | 0 | 4.7 | 0 | 0 |
| Thailand | Philippines | 3 | 0.8 | 0 | 0 |
| Singapore | Lao PDR | 1 | 2.3 | 0 | 0 |
| Cambodia | Thailand | 0.6 | 2.7 | 0 | 0 |
| China | Bangladesh | 1.2 | 1 | 0 | 0 |
| Lao PDR | Thailand | 2.3 | −0.4 | 0 | 0 |

*Note*: * Based on FDI inflow data in host economy.
*Source*: UNCTAD FDI database.

Korea, China and Malaysia, in that order. The importance of China as a source of capital is noteworthy in that there has been a great deal of debate on whether China has diverted extra-regional FDI from the rest of Southeast and East Asia.

While Hong Kong's FDI to China remained stable between the two sub-periods, that from China to Hong Kong declined. Second, intra Southeast Asia investment accounted for 6.7 percent of cumulative FDI flows in Asia between 1997 and 2005. Comparing the two sample periods, intra Southeast Asia's investment share of cumulative FDI flows in Asia increased from the first period to the next, from 4.3 percent to 7.8 percent, with Singapore as the leading investor in both periods. Singapore's investments to its ASEAN neighbours, Malaysia and Thailand, increased in the second sub-period, while the city state's investments to China and especially Hong Kong declined. Third, FDI between East Asia and South Asia remains low and stagnant.

It is important to note that the data analysed above exclude the offshore financial centers (OFCs) such as the British Virgin Islands, Bermuda, Cayman Islands, Mauritius and Western Samoa as sources of FDI. Insofar as at least some part of inflows from the OFCs involve FDI that originated from other Asian economies, and the inflows are not destined to go back to their originating country (i.e. transshipping as opposed to round-tripping), we are undercounting the size of intra-Asian FDI flows. For instance, the British Virgin Islands has consistently been the second largest source of FDI into China, surpassed only by Hong Kong, with the Cayman Islands and Western Samoa also among the top ten in 2006. Similarly, investments from other sources may have been re-routed to India via Mauritius, which has consistently been the top source of FDI to India (see Chapter 23).

Many governments in Asia have clearly taken a very positive attitude towards OFDI and have taken notable steps to liberalise capital account transactions, foreign ownership policies, foreign exchange policies and related regulations as a means of facilitating the international expansion of firms in their countries. Consequently, intra-Asian FDI flows are no longer only a North-South phenomenon but increasingly a South-South one as well, and a substantial portion of FDI from Asia is intraregional in nature.

# 23
# Revisiting India's Foreign Direct Investment Numbers[1]

*(with Sasidaran Gopalan)*

India has become increasingly important over the last decade as both a source and a host for Foreign Direct Investment (FDI) (Figure 23.1). However, trying to make sense of the numbers regarding FDI inflows and outflows can be quite challenging. The data on bilateral FDI outflows is rather sketchy; the Ministry of Finance reports the value of aggregate FDI outflows from India and the value of approvals of FDI outflows at a bilateral level, but a consistent time series of the actual value of outflows with a breakdown by country does not seem to be available in the public domain. While data on actual FDI inflows is reported by the Department of Industrial Policy and Promotion (DIPP) at a disaggregated country level, there are serious concerns about the usefulness of the bilateral FDI inflows data that is available in the public domain.

As an example, the data on FDI inflows into India almost always shows Mauritius as the largest source of foreign investment flows into the country. But Mauritius is widely regarded as an offshore financial centre (OFC) that is used by most foreign investors as an intermediary to reach India, mainly to capitalise on the tax rebates that the country offers and so minimise their overall tax burden. Conversely, as Indian companies become more globalised, many have either chosen to use their overseas locally incorporated subsidiaries to invest overseas, or have established holding companies and/or special purpose vehicles (SPVs) in OFCs or other regional financial centres such as Singapore or the Netherlands to raise funds and invest in third countries. Apart from this so-called transshipping, some parts of these inflows, from Mauritius in particular, but also from other OFCs, could also be round-tripping back to India to escape capital gains tax or for other reasons, not unlike the investment dynamics between China and Hong Kong, though on a much smaller scale (see Chapter 22). Thus, the bilateral FDI data – which only captures the actual flow of funds rather than ultimate ownership – may present a rather distorted picture of the extent of linkages between India and the rest of the world.

In order to better understand the actual or *de facto* linkages between India and the rest of the world, one would need to examine the data on actual ownership of the foreign investment flows coming into the country. While data on individual firms that have invested in India may be available via firm-level surveys, for a more complete picture of FDI inflows into the entire economy one would need to examine an aggregation of all such firms investing in India from different parts of the world. This would, however, be a prohibitively costly exercise. A more feasible alternative would be to examine the data on Mergers and Acquisitions (M&As) made by global firms in India and Indian firms globally. The M&A data, which tracks the actual ownership of the purchases and sales, is maintained by several private commercial entities, unlike the data on FDI flows, which is compiled by national sources.

Figures 23.2a and 23.2b respectively capture the data available on FDI inflows (reported by the Indian government) and the M&A purchases (reported by private commercial entities) that have taken place in India

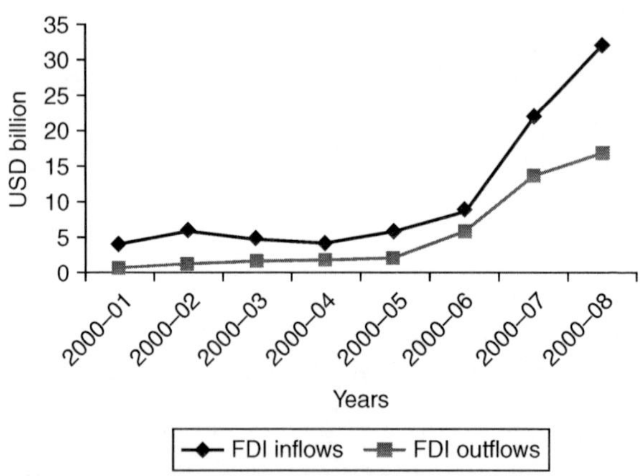


*Figure 23.1* Capital inflows to and outflows from India, 2000–08

*Source*: Based on E. Prasad (2009). "Some New Perspectives on India's Approach to Capital Account Liberalisation", Brookings India Policy Forum.

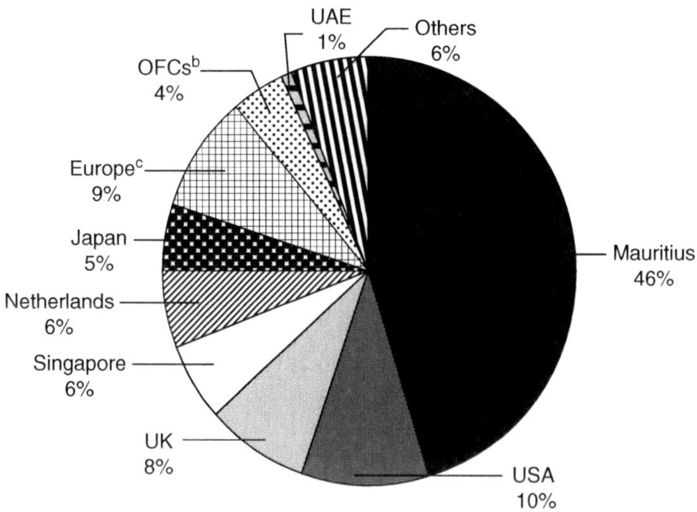


*Figure 23.2a* Share of total FDI inflows to India (percentages) by country of origin, 2000–07[a] (Top ten source countries)

*Notes*: [a]FDI data are reported for the financial year; M&A data are reported for the calendar year. [b]OFCs – Aggregation of shares of Cyprus, Channel Islands, Cayman Islands and Bermuda, excluding Mauritius. [c]Europe – Aggregation of shares of all of Europe except the Netherlands, United Kingdom and Russia.

*Source*: Ministry of Commerce and Industry, Department of Industrial Policy and Promotion (DIPP), India, http://siadipp.nic.in/publicat/newslttr/apr2008/index.htm (accessed on July 24, 2009).

(by country of origin) for the period 2000–07. A comparison of the two sets of data clearly reveals the inconsistencies discussed above . (Note: to ensure a degree of comparability with the FDI data we have only included M&As with an equity stake of over 10 percent in our direct comparisons.)

It is interesting to see that most of the OFCs, such as Mauritius (mainly) but also Cyprus, the Cayman Islands and Bermuda, which comprise nearly 50 percent of the total FDI inflows (as reported by the government sources) do not even figure in the data on inbound M&As to India. Focusing on the FDI data, only 18 percent of inflows to India have come from the US and the UK combined, while about 15 percent came from the non-UK European countries (mainly the Netherlands, France and Germany) and about 10 percent from East Asia (mainly Singapore and Japan). In contrast, the M&A data on foreign acquisitions in India tell a quite different story. The US is the single largest acquirer of Indian companies (35

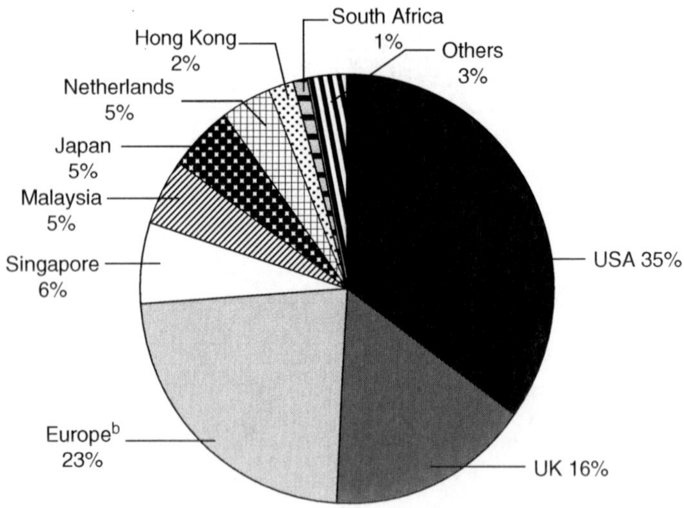


*Figure 23.2b* Share of total inbound acquisitions in India, 2000–07[a,c] (Top ten source countries) (percentages)

*Notes*: [a]FDI data are reported for the financial year; M&A data are reported for the calendar year. [b]Europe – Aggregation of shares of all of Europe except the Netherlands, United Kingdom and Russia. [c]Based on data with over 10 percent equity, for consistency with definition of FDI.

*Source*: Authors' compilations from Zephyr Database.

percent), followed by the UK (16 percent) and the rest of Europe including the Netherlands (27 percent), and East Asia (18 percent, distributed between Japan, Singapore, Malaysia and Hong Kong). So almost all of the inbound acquisitions to India have been by the US, Europe and Asia. This appears to offer a far more informative geographical breakdown of sources of direct investment equity flows to India than the FDI data.

As noted, similar bilateral data on India's actual FDI outflows are not publicly available on a systematic time series basis. While approvals may not provide a fully realistic picture, as not all approvals are realised, available data at least for aggregate actual outflows suggests that there is a reasonable degree of correlation between approved and actual outward FDI flows from India. Accordingly, the outward FDI approvals data should offer some useful insights when compared to data on India's M&A purchases overseas. It is well known that Indian businesses have been very active in overseas investments in the last few years, particularly since 2006 (Figure 23.3). Anecdotal evidence and examples point to the fact that many of these investments have been in developed

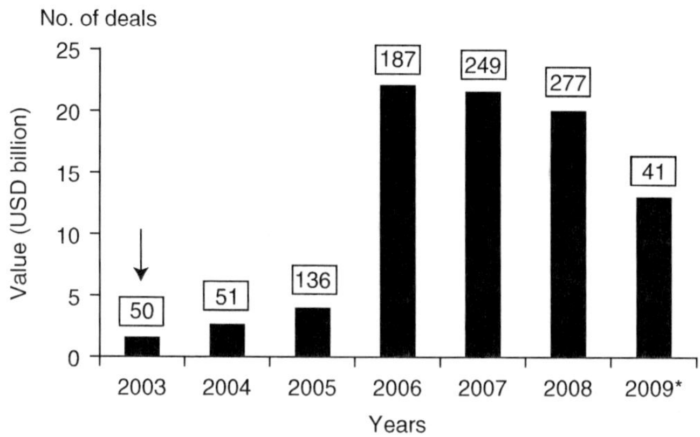


*Figure 23.3* Indian outbound mergers and acquisitions (M&As)

*Note*: * Year to date

*Source*: Reproduced from *The Economist*, May 28, 2009 based on data from Dealogic. www.economist.com/businessfinance/displaystory.cfm?story_id=13751556, (accessed on July 24, 2009).

countries such as the US, UK and the rest of Europe. Notable instances are Tata Steel's purchase of Corus, Tata Motors purchase of Jaguar and Land Rover in the UK and Hindalco's acquisition of the Canadian aluminium giant Novelis.

Referring to Figure 23.4a, one notices that developed countries such as the US and UK have surprisingly small shares of India's approved outward FDI (6 percent each) for periods for which detailed data are available (2002–08), compared to Singapore (21 percent), the Netherlands (15 percent), and Mauritius and other OFCs in total (25 percent). So over 50 percent of India's approved FDI is destined to the financial centres (regional and offshore).

Examination of M&A purchases for more or less the same period (2000–07), however, reveals quite a different picture (Figure 23.4b). Canada emerges as the top host country for India's outbound acquisitions with a 34 percent share, followed by the US with a 24 percent share. While Indian companies have undertaken a number of varied purchases in the US, acquisitions in Canada have been concentrated in resources, including Novelis, mentioned above. Apart from these, around 16 percent of India's acquisitions have been aimed at resource-rich countries (Russia, Egypt, Australia and South Africa) and the rest to the UK and Europe (17 percent). The Tata Motors acquisitions of the Jaguar and Land Rover brands from the UK do not show up in our data, as they were completed in early 2008. It is likely that an extension of

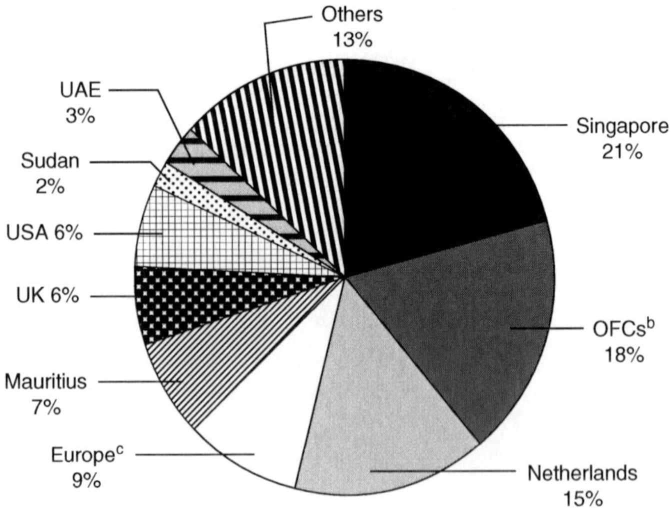


*Figure 23.4a* Share of total outward FDI approvals by India, 2002–08[a] (Top ten destination countries) (percentages)

*Notes*: [a] FDI data are reported for the financial year; M&A data are reported for the calendar year. [b] OFCs – Aggregation of shares of Cyprus, Channel Islands, Cayman Islands and Bermuda, excluding Mauritius. [c] Europe – Aggregation of shares of all of Europe except the Netherlands, UK and Russia.

*Source*: Ministry of Finance, Department of Economic Affairs http://finmin.nic.in/the_ministry/dept_eco_affairs/dea.html (accessed on July 24, 2009).

the data to 2008 would see a jump in the UK as a source of Indian outbound M&As, as would Europe in general.

One clearly has to be cautious in comparing the two sets of data (FDI versus M&A), as the M&A data excludes green field investments. While M&As are growing as the preferred mode of foreign entry, the M&A data are not from national sources, coming instead from commercial entities, and there are questions about consistency in terms of company coverage, definitions and so on. In addition, tracking transactions based on ownership is always tricky, particularly given the increasing complexity of global businesses.

That said, we can draw two basic conclusions. One, a great many acquisitions, by the US and UK in particular, have been channelled via Mauritius. Two, Indian companies have mainly been using Singapore, Netherlands and OFCs as intermediaries to purchase assets overseas, primarily in the developed world and resource-rich countries. While OFCs are used as tax havens, both Singapore and the Netherlands are

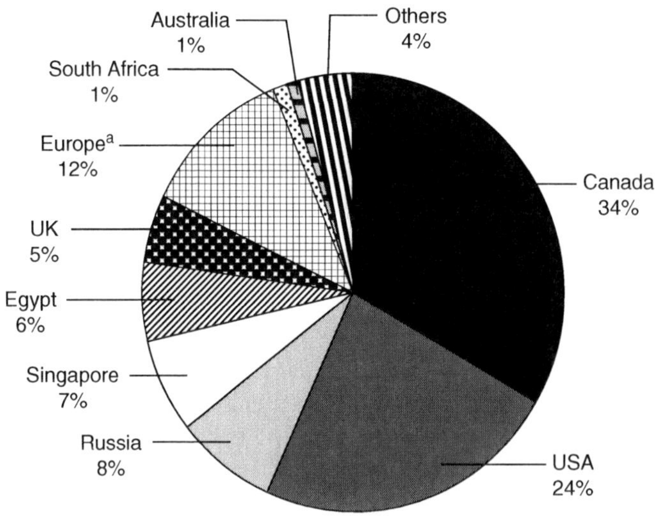


*Figure 23.4b* Share of total outbound acquisitions by India, 2000–2007[b] (Top ten destination countries) (percentages)

*Notes*: [a]Europe – Aggregation of shares of all of Europe except the Netherlands, United Kingdom and Russia. [b]Based on data with over 10 percent equity, for consistency with definition of FDI.

*Source*: Authors' compilations from Zephyr database.

attractive hosts for holding companies from India and elsewhere for (a) their low and simple tax rates, (b) the large number of double tax treaties between the two countries and the rest of the world, (c) their use of English, (d) their human capital and (e) their excellent logistics as well as air and sea connections. All this explains their attraction to Indian businesses eager to internationalise their operations.

Indian businesses have been particularly aggressive in investing in Singapore since the coming into force of the Comprehensive Economic Co-operation Agreement (CECA) in August 2005. The India-Singapore CECA, which covers agreements relating to trade in goods, services and investments, was the first bilateral arrangement that Singapore entered into with a South Asian country, and likewise India's first such agreement with a developed country. Amongst the several features of the agreement, one key provision that has assumed significance from the investment perspective is the renewed Double Taxation Avoidance Agreement (DTAA). The India-Singapore DTAA is broadly modelled on the existing Indian treaty with Mauritius, with exemptions for capital gains tax on profits from the sale of shares. Owing to the round-tripping concerns between India and Mauritius noted above, the DTAA between India and Singapore has included some key provisions to minimise this.[2]

Over time there may well be a greater shift of FDI from Mauritius to Singapore, both by Indian companies needing a springboard for investing globally, and vice versa for Singapore and other foreign companies looking to enter the Indian market. There has already been a spurt in the establishment of Indian companies in Singapore (from 1,200 in 2002 to over 3,000 by 2008),[3] and while the FDI data clearly overstates the significance of Singapore for the reasons discussed above, the city state still constitutes a substantial portion of India's overall outbound M&A (7 percent compared to 22 percent of FDI outflows from India). Apart from NatSteel's acquisition by Tata Steel in 2005, Indian educational institutions and IT companies have been prominent investors in Singapore, while many other Indian companies use Singapore as their regional or even international headquarters.

# 24

# Attracting Foreign Direct Investment: The Role of Financial and Fiscal Incentives

For decades, countries in Asia and elsewhere have competed with each other to attract FDI by offering a variety of incentives and other concessionary measures. For example, many East Asian economies have been particularly aggressive in using preferential tax treatments and other implicit and explicit subsidies to attract FDI, for example through "bidding wars" or "fiscal wars".[1]

The types of tax incentives offered by the courtier countries include reduced corporate income taxes, tax holidays, investment allowances and tax credits, accelerated depreciation allowances, exemptions from selected indirect taxes, loss carry-forwards for tax purposes and lower import tariffs on imported intermediate goods (Table 24.1). Apart from *fiscal or tax incentives,* broadly defined as policies designed primarily with a view to lower the tax burden of a firm, countries have liberally offered *financial incentives,* defined as direct transfers from the government to firms (including direct capital subsidies, subsidised loans or dedicated infrastructure). All this is done with a view to artificially increasing the rate of return or lowering the risk-adjusted costs of doing business in the country/locality.

States with stronger fiscal positions than others have used a combination of low tax rates and aggressive fiscal incentives as competitive strategies to attract FDI. For instance, Singapore has provided subsidies to investors that go well beyond traditional tax measures and involve training, expenditure, pricing of land and utilities, and even taking rather large equity stakes in selected ventures. Take the Local Industrial Upgrading Program (LIUP) of Singapore's hugely successful Economics and Development Board (EDB), for example. The aim of this scheme

*Table 24.1* Relative pros and cons of selected types of fiscal and financial incentives

| Pros | Cons |
|---|---|
| **Lower corporate income tax rate on a selective basis** | |
| • Simple to administer.<br>• Revenue costs more transparent. | • Largest benefits go to high-return firms that are likely to have invested even without incentive.<br>• Could lead to tax avoidance via transfer pricing (intracountry and international).<br>• Acts as windfall to existing investments.<br>• May not be tax-spared by home country tax authorities. |
| **Tax holidays** | |
| • Simple to administer.<br>• Allows taxpayers to avoid contact with tax administration (minimising corruption). | • Similar to lower corporate income tax rates, except that it might be tax-spared.<br>• Attracts projects of short-term maturity.<br>• Could lead to tax avoidance through the indefinite extension of holidays via "redesignation" of existing investments as new investments.<br>• Creates competitive distortions between existing and new firms.<br>• Costs are not transparent unless tax filing is required, in which case administrative benefits are foregone. |
| **Investment allowances and tax credits** | |
| • Costs are relatively transparent.<br>• Can be targeted to certain types of investment. | • Distorts the choice of capital assets towards projects of short-term maturity, since an additional allowance is available each time an asset is replaced.<br>• Qualified enterprises might attempt to abuse the system by selling and purchasing the same assets to claim multiple allowances.<br>• Greater administrative burden.<br>• Discriminates against investments with delayed returns if loss carry-forward provisions are inadequate. |

Continued

*Table 24.1* Continued

| Pros | Cons |
|---|---|
| **Lower corporate income tax rate on a selective basis** | |
| **Accelerated depreciation** | |
| • Similar benefits to investment allowances and credits.<br>• Generally does not discriminate against long-lived assets.<br>• Moves the corporate tax closer to a consumption-based tax, reducing the distortion against investment typically produced by the former. | • Some administrative burden.<br>• Discriminates against investments with delayed returns if loss carry-forward provisions are inadequate. |
| **Exemptions from indirect taxes (VAT, Import tariffs, etc.)** | |
| • Allows taxpayers to avoid contact with tax administration (minimising corruption). | • VAT exemptions may be of little benefit (under regular VAT, tax on inputs can already be credited; outputs may still get taxed at a later stage).<br>• Prone to abuse (easy to divert exempt purchases to unintended recipients). |
| **Export processing zones** | |
| • Allows taxpayers to avoid contact with tax administration (minimising corruption). | • Distorts locational decisions.<br>• Typically results in substantial leakage of untaxed goods into domestic market, eroding the tax base. |

*Source*: K. Fletcher (2002). "Tax Incentives in Cambodia, Lao PDR, and Vietnam", paper prepared for the IMF Conference on Foreign Direct Investment for Cambodia, Lao PDR and Vietnam (Hanoi, Vietnam, August 16–17) with slight modifications.

is that multinationals should help, in stages, to raise the efficiency of local suppliers. Much of the success of this scheme has been due to the financial incentives offered by the EDB in the form of the subsidising of training programmes by the EDB itself.[2]

While the theoretical literature on FDI incentives is in general fairly extensive, the empirical literature in this area has yet to catch up. However, the available empirical evidence to date suggests that such fiscal incentives may be important *at the margin* in influencing investment decisions. Incentives are particularly useful when used essentially as devices signalling the government's/country's favourable attitude towards foreign investment and the overall business environment.

Indeed, a 2000 OECD study entitled *Policy Competition for Foreign Direct Investment: A Study of Competition among Governments to Attract FDI* suggests that the investment decision-making process has two stages.[3] Investors typically begin by short-listing countries where they can invest their money on the basis of selected parameters, usually economic and political. Investment incentives do not play much of a role at this stage. It is only after the short-listing that investors consider and seek investment incentives before deciding where to invest (by playing off one potential host country against another).

From the potential host country's perspective, apart from being costly (given the tax revenues foregone as well as the costs of implementation and oversight), such incentives are least effective when used as substitutes for necessary investment-conducive policies such as disciplined macroeconomic policies, adequate infrastructural and supporting facilities, a stable and transparent regulatory environment and a relatively non-corrupt environment.

Concerns about such fiscal or financial "wars" for FDI are particularly serious in the case of larger federal countries such as Brazil, India and the US where there is a real danger of fiscal wars between states, with rents being transferred from the states to the foreign investors, to the detriment of national interests. In India, where about 80 percent of FDI inflows has been destined to just six states – Maharashtra, Gujarat, Karnataka, New Delhi, Tamil Nadu and Andhra Pradesh – other states in India have been, or may increasingly be, tempted to obtain a greater share of the FDI inflows by offering ad hoc incentives in the form of various tax concessions, subsidies, reduced power tariffs and the like, instead of tackling more fundamental factors that might hinder business activities such as poor governance and infrastructure. However, from the viewpoint of the country as a whole, broad national codes of conduct may be useful for effective and economically rational use of such incentives, as they can be a major drain on state and federal government budgets.

In the context, it is more likely than not that countries will continue to use an array of FDI incentives as part of their FDI promotional efforts, not least because the unilateral withdrawal of incentives as policy instruments by any single country might prove to be potentially costly. However, three points bear emphasis. First, the complexity and uncertainty (i.e. frequent changes) in FDI-related policies (be they incentives, taxes or laws) can have a significant deterrent effect on inflows. Second, beyond a signalling role, FDI incentives do not, by themselves, compensate for deficiencies in the overall investment climate. Third, the fiscal costs of such incentives, along with those of the investment promotion activities noted above, can be quite burdensome and must always be kept in mind when deciding if and to what extent such measures are to be utilised. The use of such incentives ought, therefore, to be guided by certain common-sense principles. Ad hoc, discretionary regimes which could give rise to rent-seeking activities should be eschewed. Focus should instead be on deploying a simple and predictable tax system with low rates for all investors, with no significant preference shown to either domestic or foreign investors (i.e. uniformity).

# 25
# Global Competition for Foreign Direct Investment and Investment Promotion

The working assumption nowadays is that in a *relatively non-distorted* domestic policy environment, FDI brings in much-needed financial capital, technical know-how, organisational, managerial and marketing practices and global production networks, thus facilitating the process of economic growth and development in host countries.[1]

Figure 25.1 shows the amounts of FDI inflows worldwide since 1990 up to the global financial crisis of 2008–09. If one looks specifically at the component for developing countries, barring a dip during 2000 and 2002, FDI has been increasing every year since 1992 despite many global uncertainties. In view of this largely benign view of FDI, there has been an intense "global race" for such forms of non-debt creating capital inflows. In fact, FDI has become one of the largest and most stable sources of external financing for most developing countries (see Chapter 20).

FDI is attracted into countries for a variety of reasons – resource-seeking (natural or human resources), market-seeking, efficiency-seeking or strategic-asset-seeking. However, at a general level, in order for a country to be more attractive to investors (both local and foreign), measures should be put in place to ensure an enabling environment. It is therefore incumbent on developing countries to take steps to ensure an enabling business environment. These steps might include enhancing inter-sectoral factor mobility (and especially reducing labour market rigidities), dismantling barriers to the free entry and exit of firms, relieving some infrastructural bottlenecks (roads, ports and storage), reducing other transaction costs of doing business (investment approvals, custom clearance, etc), including regulatory and legal impediments,

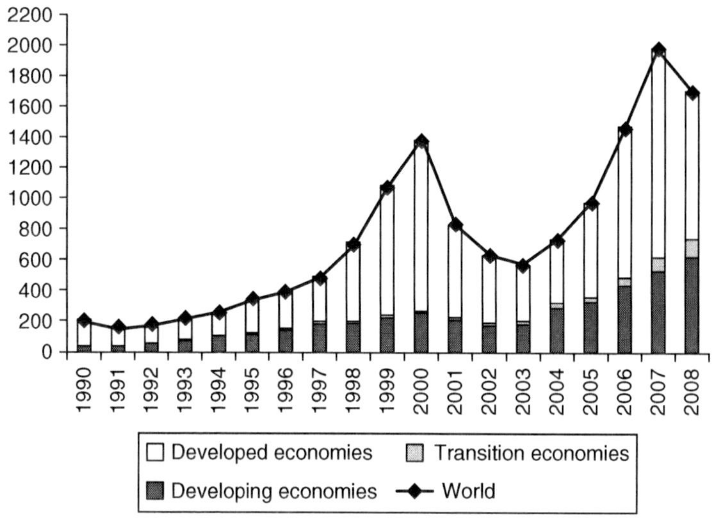


*Figure 25.1* FDI inflows, global and by groups of economies, 1990–2008 (billions of USD)

*Source*: UNCTAD FDI Statistics Online.

and strengthening overall governance (including contract enforcement) and intellectual property rights (IPRs).

Notwithstanding gradual improvements on some criteria, India continues to lag significantly behind China and many other Asian economies on most of these basic measures of business climate (as measured by the World Bank's "Doing Business" survey, for instance). Words and intentions at the federal level (statements by the Prime Minister or his colleagues or through the budget) are often not matched by deeds at the ground level, especially at the state level.

Over and above the creation of a business-friendly environment, it may be important for a potential host country to actively undertake investment promotion policies to fill in information gaps or correct the perception gaps that may hinder FDI inflows. A commonly used definition of investment promotion is that by Wells and Wint in their book *Marketing a Country: Promotion as a Tool for Attracting Foreign Investment*: "activities that disseminate information about, or attempt to create an image of the investment site and provide investment services for the prospective investors".[2]

Any investment promotion strategy must be geared towards the following: (a) image-building activities promoting the country and its regions and states as favourable locations for investment; (b) investment-generating activities through direct targeting of firms by promotion of specific sectors and industries, personal selling and establishing direct contacts with prospective investors; (c) investment-service activities tailored to prospective and current investors' needs; and (d) raising the realisation ratio (i.e. percentage of the FDI approvals translated into actual flows).

A case is often made for the establishment of a one-stop investment promotion agency (IPA) to assist in the entry and operation of FDI. The need and logic for an IPA appears to have been embraced by a number of countries, and by 2001 there were about 160 nationals IPAs and over 250 sub-national ones.[3] While a one-stop investment promotion agency could facilitate FDI by lowering administrative delays and associated cost overruns, it is important that the agency does not end up merely adding another bureaucratic layer to the process of FDI approval.

One of the few empirical analyses of IPAs in 58 countries between February and May 2002 found that there is some evidence that IPAs have a positive impact on FDI.[4] This positive impact is more likely to be felt in circumstances where IPAs (a) have a high degree of political visibility (for instance, by being linked to the highest government official such as the Prime minister's office); (b) have active private sector involvement through, for instance, participation on the IPAs board; and (c) operate in a country with a good overall investment environment. The study also finds that the types of functions that IPAs undertake have a bearing on their effectiveness (see Table 25.1 for definitions). "Policy advocacy", which is defined as steps to improve the overall investment climate and identify views of the private sector, appears to be the most effective function. This is followed by investment facilitation or servicing (the roles conventionally attributed to a one-stop shop), and image-building. IPAs seem least effective in actually generating sector-specific investments.

This suggests that growth-enhancing policy intervention probably ought *not* to have a strong sectoral bias. Instead, industrial policy should be focused on enhancing a country's general capability to benefit from FDI by (a) improving the general quality of the country's labour force and infrastructure; (b) developing local skills and technology and local learning; and (c) ensuring a stable and conducive overall macroeconomic and regulatory environment.

That said, UNCTAD continues to advocate a policy of targeted promotion, suggesting it has potentially high payoffs, though also acknowledging that it can be a risky course to take. The UNCTAD position

*Table 25.1* FDI inflows, global and by groups of economies, 1990–2008 (billions of USD)

**Image-building:** The function of creating the perception of a country as an attractive site for international investment. Activities commonly associated with image-building include focused advertising, public relations events and the generation of favourable news stories through cultivating journalists.

**Investor facilitation and investors servicing:** The range of services provided in a host country that can assist an investor in analyzing investment decisions, establishing a business, and maintaining it in good standing. Activities include information provision, "one-stop shop" service aimed at expediting approval process, utilities and various types of assistance in obtaining sites.

**Investment generation:** The targeting of specific sectors and companies with the aim of creating investment leads. Activities include the identification of potential sectors and investors, direct mailing, telephone campaigns, investor forums and seminars and individual presentations to targeted investors.

**Policy advocacy:** The activities through which the agency supports initiatives to improve the investment climate and identifies the views of the private sector on the matter. Such activities include surveys of the private sector, participation in task forces, policy and legal proposals, and lobbying.

*Source*: Reproduced with minor changes from J. Morisset (2003). "Does a Country Need a Promotion Agency to Attract Foreign Direct Investment?: A Small Analytical Model Applied to 58 Countries," Policy Research Working Paper No. 3028, The World Bank.

seems at first glance to find support from the successes of countries like Singapore whose investment promotion authority, the Economic Development Board (EDB), has very successfully targeted specific global corporations to invest in the city state and helped it industrialise in record time. Interestingly, however, even policymakers in Singapore are somewhat circumspect about the use of selective industrial promotion and targeting. As noted by a Singapore leader: "The Government can support market players where they decide it is worth basing their operations in Singapore. But we should aim to make our tax system and other incentives less targeted and more broad-based, in order to accommodate a greater degree of market experimentation, whether in manufacturing or services".[5]

More generally, the choice of the exact type and extent of such investment promotion activities and agencies must be based on a careful and systematic evaluation of potential costs and benefits. As the late Sanjaya Lall noted, "FDI strategy is an art not a science…[T]here is no ideal universal strategy on FDI. Strategy has to suit the particular conditions of the country at the particular times, and evolve as its needs change and its competitive position in the world alters."[6] Indeed, one size cannot fit all countries at all times. Particularly in cases where administrative capacity is weak, government failure is pervasive, and resources are scarce, it may be advisable for countries to avoid selective policy intervention.

# Notes

## Preface and Acknowledgements

1. Readers interested in more details on the Indian economy can refer to the following book by the author: R. S. Rajan (2009). *Monetary, Trade and Investment Issues in India*, Oxford University Press: New Delhi.

## 1 Booms and Busts in Private Capital Flows to Emerging Asia since the 1990s

1. Based on R. S. Rajan (2009). "Financial Crisis and Private Capital Flows to Emerging Economies in Asia and Elsewhere", Working Paper No. 2009–06, UN-ESCAP, December.
2. As defined by the IMF, "Emerging Asia" encompasses China, India, the newly industrialising economies (NIEs), Hong Kong, South Korea, Singapore and Taiwan, as well as the ASEAN-5 of Indonesia, Malaysia, Philippines, Thailand and Vietnam.
3. For a useful discussion of the impact of the global financial crisis on Asia and the policy responses of countries in the region, see BIS (2009), "The International Financial Crisis: Timeline, Impact and Policy Responses in Asia and the Pacific". Bank for International Settlements Office for Asia and the Pacific, August.
4. International Monetary Fund (IMF) (2009). *Global Financial Stability Report*, Washington, DC: IMF.

## 2 Asia As a Source of Capital

1. Based on R. Hattari and R. S. Rajan (2009). "Booms and Busts in Capital Flows: Asia as a Source of Capital to the US", Asian Development Bank Institute, mimeo, November.
2. The Federal Reserve Bank of New York (FRBNY) which acts a custodian for central banks, collects such data, though it does not collect private flows data. In addition, some governments may avoid the FRBNY, using private intermediaries instead.
3. For a useful overview of issues relating to the TIC data, see F. E. Warnock and V. V. Warnock (2005). "International Capital Flows and US Interest Rates", International Finance Discussion Papers No. 840, Board of Governors of the Federal Reserve System.
4. "Emerging Asia" here includes some smaller Pacific island states, but their shares are negligible.
5. India's share appears to be relatively smaller than its global share of reserves, suggesting the country's reserves are slightly more diversified than those of some of its counterparts in Asia. The purchase of gold by the RBI in

late 2009 suggests that it is looking to diversify some of its US assets even further.

6. There are some indications that China has moved towards purchasing US Treasuries of shorter-term (as opposed to long-term) maturities as well as Japanese government bonds (JGBs). See http://imarketnews.com/node/15982.

## 3 Will the US Dollar Remain the Single Global Currency?

1. For a more broad-ranging debate on the international monetary system, including the SDR, see I. M. Lago, R. Duttagupta and R. Goyal (2009). "The Debate on the International Monetary System, IMF Staff Position Note SPN/09/26", November 11.
2. For a three-stage transformation of the de facto USD reserve regime to SDRs, see P. B. Kenen (2010). "Renovation of the Global Reserve Regimes: Concepts and Proposals", Princeton University mimeo, June.
3. See B. J. Cohen (2008). "Dollar Dominance, Euro Aspirations: Recipe for Discord?", Mimeo, University of California at Santa Barbara, October.
4. For an extended analysis, see M. Jaeger (2010). "Yuan as a Reserve Currency: Likely prospects and Possible Implications", Deutsche Bank, Research, July 16.
5. M. D. Chinn. and J. Frankel (2005). "Will the Euro Surpass the Dollar as Leading International Reserve Currency", Working Paper No.11510, National Bureau of Economic Research, June.
6. "The Disappearing Dollar", *The Economist*, December 2, 2004.
7. B. Eichengreen and D. Mathieson (2000). "The Currency Composition of Foreign Exchange Reserves: Retrospect and Prospect", Working Paper No. 00/131, International Monetary Fund, p.17.
8. B. Eichengreen (2005). "Sterling's Past, Dollar's Future: Historical Perspectives on Reserve Currency Competition", Working Paper No. 11336, National Bureau of Economic Research, May.

## 4 Exchange Rate Regimes in Asia

1. Based on R. S. Rajan (2010). "The Evolution and Impact of Asian Exchange Rate Regimes", Working Paper No. 208, Asian Development Bank, July.
2. There may also be a more persistent problem of currency depreciation passing through into domestic inflation, i.e. exchange rate pass-through.
3. E. L. Levy-Yeyati and F. Struzenegger (2007). "Fear of Floating in Reverse: Exchange Rate Policy in the 2000s", mimeo.
4. V. Pontines and R. S. Rajan (2010). "Foreign Exchange Market Intervention and Reserve Accumulation in Emerging Asia: Is There Evidence of 'Fear of Appreciation'?", mimeo, January.
5. A. Subramanian (2010). "Who Pays for the Weak Renminbi?", Vox-EU, February 11, p.1.
6. H. Reisen (2010). "Global Imbalances, the Renminbi, and Poor-Country Growth", Vox-EU, November 1.

7. For an elaboration of the prisoner's dilemma in East Asia and the central role played by China, see Y. C. Park (2006). "Global Imbalances and East Asia's Policy Adjustments", mimeo, Seoul National University. As he notes:

   > There is little disagreement that an across-the-board appreciation of East Asian currencies constitutes an important component of the resolution of global imbalances. However, as noted earlier, if China insists on maintaining its limited flexibility, other East Asian countries are not likely to let their currencies strengthen vis-à-vis the Renminbi as China has emerged as their export competitor in regional as well as global markets... What is significant about China's move to an intermediate regime is that it will broaden the scope of coordination of exchange rate policy among some of the... East Asia economies and revive the discussion of establishing a new modality of cooperation for monetary integration in the region. (pp.15–16)

8. For instance, see R. S. Rajan (2002). "Exchange Rate Policy Options for Post-Crisis Southeast Asia: Is There a Case for Currency Baskets?", *The World Economy*, 25, pp.137–163.

## 5 East Asia and the Real Exchange Rate

1. Based on R. S. Rajan and J. Beverinotti (2010). "Real Exchange Rate Undervaluation, Resource Allocation and East Asian Growth", George Mason University, mimeo, July.
2. For instance, see Section 4 in S. Evenett (2010) (ed.). *The US-Sino Currency Dispute: New Insights from Economics, Politics, and Law*, VOX-EU, April.
3. "US House passes China currency sanctions bill", BBC, September 29, 2010. (www.bbc.co.uk/news/business-11437808); For instance, see S. Evenett (2010) (ed.), *ibid.*, sections 1 and 5.
4. We use the terms of trade and current account imbalances interchangeably, effectively ignoring factor payments and interest income.
5. Anecdotal evidence pointing to wage-price pressures and labour unrest in China is growing. For instance, see A. Peaple (2010). "China's Rising Workers", *Wall Street Journal*, May 31. For more systematic evidence on China's real wage rates, see D. Tao Yang, V. Chen and R. Monarch (2009). "Rising Wages: Has China Lost Its Global Labor Advantage?", mimeo, The Conference Board, New York.
6. D. Rodrik (2008). "The Real Exchange Rate and Economic Growth", *Brookings Papers on Economic Activity*, Fall, pp.365–412.
7. Ibid.
8. For a discussion on structural reforms needed in China, see Y. Huang and K. Tao (2010). "Causes and Remedies of China's External Imbalances", Working Paper No. E2010002, China Center for Economic Research, Peking University, Beijing. For a comprehensive discussion of China's savings rate, see G. Ma and Y. Wang (2010). "The Evolving Role of China in the Global Economy", paper presented at *CESifo* Venice Summer Institute, July 19–24, 2010.
9. See the People's Bank of China: www.pbc.gov.cn/english/detail.asp?col=6400&id=1488. It is important to keep in mind that China did make a similar announcement on July 21, 2005, when it started allowing the RMB to

gradually appreciate vis-à-vis the US dollar. That policy was put on hold from July 2008, when China returned to a firm US dollar peg with the onset of the global financial crisis, because of concerns about export and growth slowdown and global deflation. For an empirical evaluation of China's exchange rate regime, see J. A. Frankel (2009). "New Estimation of China's Exchange Rate Regime", Working Paper No. 14700, National Bureau of Economic Research, February.

10. China runs a trade deficit with East Asian neighbours such as Japan and Korea. In fact, in March 2010 China ran an aggregate trade deficit, its surpluses vis-à-vis the US and the EU being offset by trade deficits with Asia and elsewhere. www.chinadaily.com.cn/bizchina/2010-04/10/content_9711353.htm.
11. International Monetary Fund (IMF) (2010). *World Economic Outlook: Rebalancing Growth*, IMF: Washington, DC (April). Chapter 4 discusses the Plaza Accord and the impact of currency account surpluses reversals in Japan and elsewhere.
12. For a discussion of trajectories on US fiscal deficit and debt, see D. W. Elmendorf (2010). "US Fiscal Policy after the Financial Crisis and Recession", presentation to the International Monetary Fund Fiscal Forum, April 23.

## 6 The Problem with Exchange Rate Volatility

1. Based on R. S. Rajan (2010). "The Evolution and Impact of Asian Exchange Rate Regimes", Working Paper No. 208, Asian Development Bank, July.
2. For instance, an IMF study of 123 emerging economies covering the period 1975–96 found the median inflation rate of "peggers" to be consistently lower and less volatile than those with more flexible arrangements, though the inflation rate differential between the two sets of countries has decreased through the 1990s. See International Monetary Fund (IMF) (1997). *World Economic Outlook*, Washington, DC: IMF.
3. J. Shambaugh (2004). "The Effects of Fixed Exchange Rates on Monetary Policy", *Quarterly Journal of Economics*, 119, pp.300–351.
4. A. Di Giovanni. and J. Shambaugh (2005). "The Impact of Foreign Interest Rates on the Economy: The Role of the Exchange Rate Regime", Working Paper No. 06/37, International Monetary Fund, November.
5. There may even be a degree of endogeneity in the sense that as countries "learn to float", they gain a greater degree of monetary policy autonomy. Of course, if unrestrained monetary policy has been a facet of a country's past, imposing exchange rate fixity may be an advantage, as it constrains the active use of monetary policy.
6. M. McKenzie (1999). "The Impact of Exchange Rate Volatility on International Trade Flows", *Journal of Economic Surveys*, 13, pp.71–103. In another recent review of exchange rates, the author concludes:

    The main conclusion of this note is that there is a case for policy to stabilise exchange rates. Large fluctuations in exchange rates – even if they are not "excessive" fluctuations due to market sentiment or bubbles – can lead to inefficient allocation of resources. Unperturbed free markets in foreign exchange cannot be relied upon to arrive at exchange rate levels that deliver terms of trade and real exchange rates that reflect the underlying economic productivity, efficiency, and competitiveness of economies. (p.246)

See C. Engel (2010). "Exchange Rate Policies", The International Financial Crisis and Policy Challenges in Asia and the Pacific, BIS Papers No 52, July, pp.220–250.

7. A. Bénassy-Quéré,, L. Fontagné and A. Lahrèche-Révil (2001). "Exchange Rate Strategies in the Competition for Attracting FDI", *Journal of the Japanese and International Economies*, 15, pp.178–198.
8. There are technical issues in terms of how exchange rate volatility is measured; whether certain outliers drive the results; differentiating between volatility and valuations; the underlying causes of volatility, and so on. For instance, the IMF undertook a comprehensive analysis of exchange rate volatility and trade. It examined exchange rate variability over the preceding thirty years for all countries and reached the following conclusion:

   [T]he current study does not find a robustly negative effect. To be more precise, the study reports some evidence that is consistent with a negative effect of volatility on trade. However, such a relationship is not robust to certain reasonable perturbation of the specification... Changes in the volatility of the exchange rate may reflect changes in the volatility of the underlying shocks and/or changes in the policy regime. For example, trade liberalisation undertaken together with a move to greater exchange rate flexibility could well be associated with increased trade flows as well as increased exchange rate volatility. This possibility is a reason for the ambiguity of the theoretical results as well as the difficulty in finding consistent and robust empirical results regarding the impact of volatility on trade. An additional implication is that the empirical results do not provide clear policy guidance... There do not appear to be strong grounds to take measures to reduce exchange rate movements from the perspective of promoting trade flow.

   See P. Clark, N. Tamirisa and S. J. Wei with A. Sadikov and Z. Li (2004). "Exchange Rate Volatility and Trade Flows – Some New Evidence", mimeo, IMF.
9. This finding, while interesting, is limited to a single year (2005) based on data from CEPII-CHELEM database for ASEAN-5 plus China, Japan and South Korea. See W. Thorbecke (2008). "The Effect of Exchange Rate Volatility on Fragmentation in East Asia: Evidence from the Electronics Industry", *Journal of the Japanese and International Economies*, 22, pp.535–544.
10. This apart, the IMF economists note the need for an alternative nominal anchor, formulation of intervention policies and ensuring managing exchange rate risks. See I. Ötker-Robe and D. Vavra et al. (2007). "Moving to Greater Exchange Rate Flexibility: Operations Aspects Based on Lessons from Detailed Country Experiences", Occasional Paper No. 256, IMF.
11. W. M. Corden (2003). *Too Sensational on the Choice of Exchange Rate Regimes*, Cambridge, MA: MIT Press.

## 7 Capital Controls: No Longer Unorthodox

1. For up-to-date descriptions of Asian capital controls, see C. Chan. S. Flint, P. Pande and P. Gupta (2010). "Currency Wars – Asia and the Risk of Capital Controls", Nomura FX Insights, October 7 and Y. Khatri, E. Paracuelles and

R. Subbaraman (2010). "The Case for Capital Controls", Asia Special Report, Nomura Global Economics, November 1.
2. See Chapter 15 of this volume for a discussion of G20 issues.
3. J. D. Ostry, A. R. Ghosh, K. Habermeier, M. Chamon, M. S. Qureshi, and D. B. S. Reinhardt (2010). "Capital Inflows: the Role of Controls", Staff Position Papers SPN/10/04, IMF.
4. Specifically, the ADB has noted:

    > Capital controls against volatile short-term inflows can safeguard macroeconomic stability and facilitate the transition to more flexible exchange rates. In contrast to long-term capital inflows such as FDI, short-term capital flows are often volatile and disruptive. They can cause overheating pressures and their sudden reversal can wreak financial havoc. Short-term inflows can also lead to sharp currency appreciation, thereby eroding a country's competitiveness. Such episodes can decelerate the momentum toward greater exchange rate flexibility. However, capital controls should be selective, and targeted toward potentially more destabilizing types of inflows. In light of the well known distortions and efficiency costs that they introduce, capital controls should be gradually withdrawn as a country reaches higher levels of financial development. Easing restrictions on capital outflows could be another option to redress the adverse impact of speculative capital inflows. (p.94)

    See ADB (2010). *Asian Development Outlook 2010*, Asian Development Bank.
5. For a more exhaustive list of possible forms of controls on capital and current account transactions, see the latest country survey in the IMF's *Exchange Rate Arrangements and Exchange Restrictions Annual Report*, Washington, DC: IMF. http://www.imf.org/external/np/mfd/er/index.asp
6. For instance, see B. Eichengreen, M. Mussa, G. Dell'Ariccia, E. Detragiache, G. Milesi-Ferretti, (1999). "Liberalizing Capital Movements: Some Analytical Issues", Economic Issues No. 17, February.
7. D. Mathieson and L. Rojas-Suarez (1993). "Liberalization of the Capital Account: Experiences ad Issues", Occasional Paper No. 103, International Monetary Fund.
8. K. J. Forbes (2003). "One Cost of the Chilean Capital Controls: Increased Financial Constraints for Small Traded Firms", Working Paper No. 9777, National Bureau of Economic Research, June.

## 8 Reconsidering the Tobin Tax

1. See Bank for International Settlements (BIS) (2007). "Foreign Exchange and Derivatives Market Activity in 2007", *Triennial Central Bank Survey*, December.
2. R. Dornbusch (1998). "Capital Controls: an Idea Whose Time is Gone", *Essays in International Finance No. 207*, International Economics Section, Princeton University, p.2.
3. See the following website dedicated to the Tobin tax: www.ceedweb.org/iirp/

## 9 Sovereign Debt Defaults: Concerns and Lessons

1. www.icrier.org/pdf/OP02SovDebt.pdf
2. *Ibid.*

3. www.imf.org/external/pubs/ft/survey/so/2007/POL0511A.htm
4. *Ibid.*
5. www.businessweek.com/ap/financialnews/D9I53A880.htm.
6. For analyses of the Greek crisis and policy options, see www.voxeu.com/index.php?q=node/5034.

## 10 Banking Sector Internationalisation in Asia

1. Based on S. Gopalan and R. S. Rajan (2009). "Financial Sector De-Regulation in Asia: Focus on Foreign Bank Entry", Working Paper No. 76, Institute of South Asian Studies, Singapore, July.
2. S. Claessens, A. Demirgüç-Kunt and H. Huizinga (1998), "How Does Foreign Entry Affect the Domestic Banking Market?", Policy Research Working Paper No. 1918, The World Bank, June.
3. However, recent experiences have given policymakers and observers some reason to revisit this oft-noted advantage of foreign bank entry; we return to this issue later in the chapter.
4. Data for foreign bank assets are more easily available and hence more complete (and probably more accurate) than those for foreign bank deposits.
5. That said, much more research is needed on the relative costs and benefits of branches versus subsidiaries, the latter being relatively independent from the parent. For instance, are the former more likely to be supported by their parent in the event of a crisis in the host country but also more likely to "cut and run" in the event of a crisis in the source country or a global crisis?

## 11 The Global Financial Crisis of 2008–2009: Implications for Emerging Asia

1. Based on R. S. Rajan (2009). "Financial Crisis and Private Capital Flows to Emerging Economies in Asia and Elsewhere", Working Paper No. 2009–06, UN-ESCAP, December.
2. Asian Development Bank (ADB) (2009). *Asian Development Outlook 2009*, Manila: ADB, p.28.
3. International Monetary Fund IMF (2009a). *Regional Economic Outlook – Asia and Pacific Global Crisis: The Asian Context*, Washington, DC: IMF.
4. For more details on the ways in which Asia was impacted and the policy responses to the crisis, see International Monetary Fund (2009b). *Global Financial Stability Report*, Washington, DC: IMF.
5. The data should be taken as indicative only, given that the 2009 forecasts for the whole year were as of July 2009; things improved far more robustly in the third and fourth quarters of 2009.
6. IMF (2009b), *op. cit.*, p.2.
7. IMF (2009a) explores the resiliency of the Asian corporate sector.

## 12 Sequencing of Regional Cooperation in Asia: The Real and Financial Dimensions

1. See R. S. Rajan (2005). "Asian Economic Cooperation and Integration: Sequencing of Financial, Trade and Monetary Regionalism", in *Asian Economic*

*Cooperation and Integration: Progress, Prospects and Challenges*, Manila: Asian Development Bank.

2. The term "regionalism" is used in this chapter in a completely neutral manner. It is not intended to imply that the region is "inward-looking" or "protectionist" (i.e. no "fortress Asia").
3. We do not consider regional cooperation and integration in other areas, including energy, technology and skills training, and infrastructure and transportation. For a broad overview of these issues, see N. Kumar (2002). "Towards an Asian Economic Community-Vision of Closer Economic Cooperation in Asia: An Overview", RIS Discussion Paper No.32, Research and Information Systems for the Non-Aligned and Developing Countries (RIS), New Delhi, India.
4. For an overview of Asian FTAs, see M. Kawai and G. Wignaraja (2009). "Asian FTAs: Trends and Challenges", Working Paper No. 144, Asian Development Bank Institute, September.
5. The EMEAP is "a cooperative organisation of central banks and monetary authorities (hereinafter simply referred to as central banks) in the East Asia and Pacific region. Its primary objective is to strengthen the cooperative relationship among its members. It comprises the central banks of eleven economies: Reserve Bank of Australia, People's Bank of China, Hong Kong Monetary Authority, Bank Indonesia, Bank of Japan, Bank of Korea, Bank Negara Malaysia, Reserve Bank of New Zealand, Bangko Sentral ng Pilipinas, Monetary Authority of Singapore, and Bank of Thailand." See www.emeap.org.
6. More information on all these and other initiatives is available on the portal created and maintained by the Asian Development Bank (ADB) http://asianbondsonline.adb.org/.
7. For details on the ABF, see R. S. Rajan (2008). "Monetary and Financial Cooperation in Asia: Taking Stock of Recent On-goings", *International Relations of the Asia-Pacific*, 8, pp.31–45 and G. Ma and E. M. Remolona (2005). "Opening Markets through a Regional Bond Fund: Lessons from ABF2", *BIS Quarterly Review*, June, pp.81–92.
8. Y. Jinjarak (2004). "On the Hidden Links between Financing Costs and International Trade Patterns", mimeo, June.
9. The FDI-trade nexus is outlined by Kawai (2005). "Trade and Investment Cooperation and Integration in Asia: Empirical Evidence and Issues", *Asian Economic Cooperation and Integration*, in *Asian Economic Cooperation and Integration: Progress, Prospects and Challenges*, Manila: Asian Development Bank.
10. As a rule of thumb, in the case of emerging economies in Asia, equity financing usually contributes about a quarter of total project cost, the remainder being financed by lending (usually bank lending but increasingly via bond financing).
11. See K. Forbes and M. Chinn (2004). "A Decomposition of Global Linkages in Financial Markets Over Time", *The Review of Economics and Statistics*, 86, pp.705–722.
12. Indeed, it is unclear even whether some forms of stronger financial cooperation, such as standard harmonization, ought to be done at the regional level, many arguing that the region should aim for international rather than regional standards.

13. For a discussion of OCA criteria, see T. D. Willett (2001). "The OCA Approach to Exchange Rate Regimes: A Perspective on Recent Developments", mimeo, Claremont Colleges.
14. R. Mundell (1973). "Uncommon Arguments for Common Currencies", in H. Johnson and A. Swoboda (eds.), *The Economics of Common Currencies*, London: Allen and Unwin.
15. This argument is elaborated in R. McKinnon (1963). "Optimum Currency Areas", *American Economic Review*, 53, pp.717–725 and J. Frankel and A. Rose (2002). "An Estimate of the Effect of Currency Unions on Trade and Growth", *Quarterly Journal of Economics*, 117, pp.437–466.
16. See P. Krugman (1993). "Lessons of Massachusetts for EMU", in F. Torres and F. Giavazzi (eds.), *Adjustment and Growth in the European Monetary Union*, Cambridge, UK: Cambridge University Press and B. Eichengreen (1992)."Should the Maastricht Treaty Be Saved?", *Princeton Studies in International Finance No.64*, International Economics Section, Princeton University.
17. C. A. Calderón, A. Chong and E. Stein (2002). "Trade Intensity and Business Cycle Synchronization: Are Developing Countries any Different?", Working Paper No. 195, Central Bank of Chile, December.
18. Y. F. L. Lee (2004). "Trade, Business Cycles, and the Optimum Currency Area", Economics Discussion Papers, Southern Illinois University Carbondale, mimeo, February.
19. S. Kalemi-Ozcan, B. Sorensen and O. Yosha, (2001). "Economic Integration, Industrial Specialization and the Asymmetry of Shocks Across Regions", *Journal of International Economics*, 55, pp.107–137 and S. Kalemi-Ozcan, B. Sorensen and O. Yosha (2003). "Risk Sharing and Industrial Specialization: Regional and International Evidence", *American Economic Review*, 93, pp.903–918.
20. In fact some have argued that financial liberalisation by (East) Asian economies has led to intensified *international* rather than *regional* integration. Part of the reason for the differing experience of Asia and Europe may be because of the policy decision within the EU to harmonise national financial regulations *prior to* financial liberalisation. In contrast, regional financial integration in East Asia may have been hindered by the absence of relevant market-supporting infrastructure. See B. Eichengreen. and Y. C. Park (2003). "Financial Liberalization and Capital Market Integration in East Asia", mimeo, undated.
21. Studies in this area were pioneered by Andrew Rose, who has gone on to write a number of papers in the area. See http://faculty.haas.berkeley.edu/arose/RecRes.htm
22. For instance, see J. P. Danthine, F. Giavazzi and E. L. von Thadden (2000). "European Financial Markets After EMU: A First Assessment", mimeo, May. However, the reverse causation may also be true, i.e. "it is the more advanced development of European capital markets and institutions in the period leading up to the removal of financial restrictions and capital controls that caused Europe to respond to developing deeper financial links within the region as well as globally". See B. Eichengreen. and Y. C. Park (2003), *op. cit.*

23. As elaborated upon by J. Frankel and A. Rose (1998). "The Endongeneity of the Optimum Currency Area Criteria", *Economic Journal*, 108, pp.1009–1025.
24. E. Fernandez-Arias, U. Panizza and E. Stein (2002). "Trade Agreements and Exchange Rate Disagreements", Inter-American Development Bank, mimeo, March.
25. B. Eichengreen (2002a). "What Macroeconomic Measures are Needed for Free Trade to Flourish in the Western Hemisphere?", mimeo, November.
26. For a detailed discussion of preconditions for an AMU, see B. Eichengreen. (2005). "Real and Pseudo Preconditions for an Asian Monetary Union", in *Monetary and Financial Cooperation in East Asia*, Palgrave-McMillan Press for the Asian Development Bank.
27. For an elaboration, see T. Ito (2003). "The ABC of Asian Bonds", paper presented at the Second PECC Finance Forum Conference, Hua Hin, Thailand, July 8–9.

## 13 Revisiting Asian Monetary and Financial Cooperation

1. This suggests a degree of exchange rate asymmetry in their exchange rate policies, i.e. so-called "fear of appreciation", not "fear of floating" per se; see Chapter 6.
2. For an elaboration of the issue of regional surveillance in Asia, see E. Girardin (2004). "Information Exchange, Surveillance Systems, and Regional Institutions in East Asia", in *Monetary and Financial Integration in East Asia*, Palgrave Macmillan for the Asian Development Bank.
3. For details, see R. Siregar and R. S. Rajan (2004). "Centralized Reserve Pooling for the ASEAN Plus Three (APT) Countries", in *Monetary and Financial Cooperation in East Asia*, Palgrave Macmillan for the Asian Development Bank.
4. For a useful overview of the design of regional surveillance in Asia, see S. Takagi (2010). "Regional Surveillance for East Asia: How Can It Be Designed to Complement Global Surveillance", Working Paper Series on Regional Economic Integration No.50, Asian Development Bank, May.
5. The APT members have announced that an ASEAN Plus Three Macroeconomic Research Office (AMRO) will be established in Singapore by mid 2011. See: www.aseansec.org/19588.htm

## 14 The Idea and Reality of the Asian Currency Unit (ACU)

1. Based on R. S. Rajan (2009). "Financial Crisis and Private Capital Flows to Emerging Economies in Asia and Elsewhere", Working Paper No. 2009-06, UN-ESCAP, December.
2. Based on V. Pontines and R. S. Rajan (2008). "The Asian Currency Unit (ACU): Exploring Alternative Currency Weights", *Macroeconomics and Finance in Emerging Market Economies*, 1, pp.269–278.
3. H. Kuroda (2005). "Towards a borderless Asia: a perspective on Asian economic integration", speech by Asian Development Bank (ADB) President at the Emerging Markets Forum (December 10, Oxford).

4. See S. Watanabe and M. Ogura (2006). "How Far Apart Are Two ACUs from Each Other? Asian Currency Unit and Asian Currency Union", Working Paper No. 06-E-20, Bank of Japan, November.

## 15 Asia in the G20: Monetary and Financial Considerations

1. Apart from the G-8 members, the EU and Australia, the other (emerging economy) members of the G20 are Argentina, Brazil, China, India, Indonesia, South Korea, Mexico, South Africa, Saudi Arabia and Turkey.
2. The FSB has the following members – all G20 countries, Spain, Hong Kong, Netherlands; Singapore, Switzerland, the UK and the US. For a detailed discussion of the FSB, see S. Griffith-Jones, E. Helleiner and N. Woods (2010). "The Financial Stability Board: an Effective Fourth Pillar of Global Economic Governance?" Center for International Governance Innovation, Canada. Available at www.cigionline.org/sites/default/files/FSB%20special%20 report_2.pdf.
3. A critical overview of the "failure of the G20" can be found here. www.coc.org/node/6370; Also see www.eurodad.org/whatsnew/articles.aspx?id=3603;
4. J. Lipsky (2010). "The G20 Agenda: Looking to Seoul", remarks by John Lipsky, First Deputy Managing Director, International Monetary Fund, delivered at the Korea Economic Institute, Washington, DC, July 27.
5. See E. M. Truman (2010). "The G20 and International Financial Institution Governance", Working Paper No.10–13, Peterson Institute, September.
6. See www.imf.org/external/pubs/ft/survey/so/2010/NEW102310A.htm.
7. A cynical view is that some of the emerging economies are just content that they have been invited to the table and have given little thought to what they want to achieve at the forum, let alone take a leadership position.
8. For a discussion of G20's legitimacy deficit and an elaboration of the role of Singapore and the Global Governance Group (3G), see I. A. Chowdhury (2010). "The Global Governance Group ('3G') and Singaporean Leadership: Can Small be Significant?", Working Paper No.108, Institute of South Asian Studies, Singapore, May 19.
9. However, the fact that India supported the US position on the Chinese currency (revaluation) issue before the G20 meeting of Finance Ministers and Central Bank Governors in April 2010 in Washington DC could cast a shadow on the extent of cooperation within the East Asian caucus.

## 16 The Global Financial Crisis and the Bank Lending Channel

1. Based on M. S. Islam and R. S. Rajan (2010). "Bank Lending Channel of Monetary Policy Transmission: India and the Global Financial Crisis", Working Paper No. 78, Institute of South Asian Studies, Singapore, July.
2. The repo rate is the rate at which commercial banks borrow money from the RBI. This is the rate at which the central bank provides liquidity to the

banks. The reverse repo rate, on the other hand, is the rate at which the RBI borrows money from the commercial banks to drain excess liquidity out of the system.

3. The public sector banks in India accounted for 69.9, 73.9 and 72.6 percent of assets, deposits and loans in 2007–08. See Reserve Bank of India (2009). *Macroeconomic and Monetary Development*, RBI: Mumbai. Also see Chapter 10.

## 17 Macroeconomic Management during a Period of Plenty in India

1. www.piie.com/events/event_detail.cfm?EventID=151. Also see T. Baig and K. Das (2010). Rupee and Capital Controls", Deutsche Bank Asia Economics Special, October 21.

## 18 Post-Global Financial Crisis: Heating Up of the Inflation Debate in India

1. The new WPI series with the base year 2004–05 has been published since August 2010.
2. Figures based on the new series of the WPI. According to the old series with a 1993–94 base, inflation rose 9.5 percent in August 2010, down from 9.7 percent in July. The rise in August was the slowest in seven months.
3. www.eastasiaforum.org/2010/09/24/india-and-the-scourge-of-relentless-inflation/; Overall, between 2006 and June 2010, the repo and reverse repo rates have come down, while CRR has experienced an increase. The reverse repo rate had been more or less constant until the end of 2008, after which it dropped steeply and was at its lowest since 2006, until the beginning of this year, when the RBI started raising these rates to control rising inflation in the country. The repo rates rose from 2006 to the end of 2008, after which the RBI reduced them and has increased them since the beginning of 2010 to combat inflation. The CRR also followed a similar trend, though it experienced an increase overall from 2006.
4. Refer note 2 in Chapter 16.
5. http://rbidocs.rbi.org.in/rdocs/notification/PDFs/FMDCIRD1692010.pdf; www.rbi.org.in/scripts/BS_PressReleaseDisplay.aspx?prid=23134.
6. Dr. D. Subbarao (2010). "Financial Crisis – Some Old Questions and Maybe Some New Answers". Tenth C. D. Deshmukh Memorial Lecture delivered by Dr. D. Subbarao, Governor, Reserve Bank of India, at the Council for Social Development, Southern Regional Centre (Hyderabad, August 5, 2010).

## 19 India's International Reserves: How Diversified?

1. Based on R. S. Rajan and S. Gopalan (2010). "India's Reserves: How Large? How Diversified?", Working Paper No. 104, Institute of South Asian Studies, Singapore, March.
2. R. S. Rajan and S. Gopalan (2010), *op. cit.*

## 20 The Importance of Remittances in India and South Asia

1. Based on S. Gopalan and R. S. Rajan (2010). "External Financing in South Asia: The Remittances Option", *ARTNET Policy Brief No. 23*, UN-ESCAP, Thailand, January 23.
2. World Bank (2008), available at http://go.worldbank.org/T0TEVOV4E0.
3. See World Bank (2010). *Global Development Finance 2010*, World Bank: Washington D.C.
4. World Bank (2009). *Global Development Finance 2009*, World Bank: Washington D.C.
5. A caveat needs to be borne in mind. When one considers all the seven South Asian countries, Nepal emerges as the highest recipient of remittances in the region, with a share of over 15 percent of the country's GDP in 2007 (World Development Indicators Online). But due to limited data availability on Nepal's other types of private sources of financing, we have excluded the country from our analysis.
6. World Bank (2006): Global Economic Prospects 2006: Economic Implications of Remittances and Migration, World Bank: Washington DC.
7. CVs become less effective (and misleading) as a measure of (in) stability if there is a trend in the data. Thus it is inadvisable to use them for longer time periods when series have unit roots.
8. We confine the period to 2000 and 2007 for calculating CVs for the cluster of developing countries as a whole.
9. It is worth noting that there is a small but growing body of empirical work confirming the presence of *counter-cyclical* behaviour of remittances, though much more work remains to be done in this area. For instance, see J. Frankel (2009). "Are Bilateral Remittances Counter Cyclical?" Center for International Development, Harvard University.
10. Some have argued that the large inflows of remittances into a particular country could result in a "Dutch Disease" type of situation, where the recipient country experiences an overvalued real exchange rate (due to an appreciation or strengthening of its currency), which would lead to a loss of export competitiveness, which would in turn make the production of such tradable goods less profitable. However, there are a growing number of empirical studies that seem to suggest that this concern is misplaced. For an overview, see World Bank (2006). *Global Economic Prospects 2006: Economic Implications of Remittances and Migration*, World Bank: Washington D.C.

## 21 Foreign Portfolio versus Foreign Direct Investment Flows: Are They So Different?

1. Based on R. Hattari and R. S. Rajan (2010). How Different are FDI and FPI Flows?: Does Distance Alter the Composition of Capital Flows?", Working Paper, Hong Kong for Monetary Research, forthcoming.

2. Thus, FDI and FPI may be negatively correlated if there is a fire-sale of assets during a crisis and foreign investors who have bought controlling equity stakes then turn around and sell part of their stake following asset price revaluations once the crisis abates. See V. Acharya, H. S. Shin and T. Yorulmazer (2008). Fire-Sale FDI, mimeo, Princeton University and G. Bird and R. S. Rajan (2002). "Financial Crises and the Composition of International Capital Flows: Does FDI Guarantee Stability?", *Development Policy Review*, 20, pp.191–202.
3. See www.treas.gov/offices/international-affairs/exon-florio/. For a discussion of China's SWF investments, see M. F. Martin (2008). "China's Sovereign Wealth Fund", CRS Report for Congress, January 22. The author has also emphasised that China's decision to purchase something less than 10 percent of Blackstone's shares was apparently not arbitrary and that there was a strategic reason behind it. As he notes, according to Blackstone's CEO and Chairman Stephen A. Schwarzman, "The deal is 'purely commercial' and do [sic] not need the U.S. government approval as the stake is less than 10 percent" (p.8). The Chinese investment was later increased to a 12.5 percent stake.

## 22 Intra-Asian Foreign Direct Investment Flows

1. Based on. R. Hattari and R. S. Rajan (2008). "Trends and Drivers of Bilateral FDI Flows in Developing Asia", Working Papers No. 112008, Hong Kong Institute for Monetary Research, November.
2. UNCTAD (2006). *World Investment Report 2006*, New York and Geneva: United Nations, p.6
3. World Bank (2006). *Global Development Finance*. New York: Oxford University Press.
4. Accenture (2005) *China Spreads its Wings – Chinese Companies go Global*. Accenture.
5. UNCTAD (2006), *op. cit.*, chapter 2.

## 23 Revisiting India's Foreign Direct Investment Numbers

1. Based on S. Gopalan and R. S. Rajan (2010). "India's FDI Flows: Trying to Make Sense of the Numbers", *ARTNET Alerts*, Issue 5, UN-ESCAP, Thailand, January.
2. For more details on the key provisions of the India-Singapore CECA, see http://app-stg.mti.gov.sg/data/article/116/doc/FTA_CECA_Information%20 Kit.pdf
3. See http://in.rediff.com/money/2008/mar/19india.htm.

## 24 Attracting Foreign Direct Investment: The Role of Financial and Fiscal Incentives

1. See R. S. Rajan (2005). "FDI, Trade and the Internationalization of Production in the Asia-Pacific Region", Asia-Pacific Trade and Investment Review, 1, pp.3–26.

2. For instance, see C. P. Oman (2000). *Policy Competition for Foreign Direct Investment: A Study of Competition Among Governments to Attract FDI*, OECD Development Centre: Paris, chapter 2.
3. Oman, *ibid.*

## 25 Global Competition for Foreign Direct Investment and Investment Promotion

1. See R. S. Rajan (2005). "FDI, Trade and the Internationalization of Production in the Asia-Pacific Region", Asia-Pacific Trade and Investment Review, 1, pp.3–26.
2. L. Wells Jr. and A. Wint (1990). *Marketing a Country: Promotion as a Tool for Attracting Foreign Investment*, IFC and MIGA: Washington, DC.
3. UNCTAD (2001). "The World of Investment Promotion at a Glance: A Survey of Investment Promotion Practices", *United Nations Advisory Studies No. 17*, UNCTAD/ITE/IPC/3, New York and Geneva.
4. J. Morisset and O. L. Neso (2002). "Administrative Barriers to Foreign Investment in Developing Countries", *Transnational Corporations*, 11, pp.99–121.
5. Speech by Mr Tharman Shanmugaratnam (2002). "Succeeding in an Unpredictable World – Moving from a Managed to an Entrepreneurial Economy", at the Singapore 1000/SME 500 Awards Ceremony (Singapore, January 18, 2002).
6. S. Lall (2000). "FDI and Development: Policy and Research Issues in the Emerging Context", Working Paper No. 43, Queen Elizabeth House, University of Oxford, June, pp.20–21.

# Subject Index